OPPOSING VIEWPOINTS® SERIES

Epidemics

Other Books of Related Interest:

Opposing Viewpoints Series

Antibiotics

Obesity

Health

At Issue Series

Are Americans Overmedicated?

The H1N1 Flu

AIDS in Developing Countries

Current Controversies Series

Disease Eradication

Medical Ethics

"Congress shall make no law ... abridging the freedom of speech, or of the press."

First Amendment to the U.S. Constitution

The basic foundation of our democracy is the First Amendment guarantee of freedom of expression. The Opposing Viewpoints Series is dedicated to the concept of this basic freedom and the idea that it is more important to practice it than to enshrine it.

OPPOSING VIEWPOINTS® SERIES

Epidemics

David Haugen and Susan Musser, Book Editors

GREENHAVEN PRESS
A part of Gale, Cengage Learning

GALE
CENGAGE Learning™

Detroit • New York • San Francisco • New Haven, Conn • Waterville, Maine • London

Christine Nasso, *Publisher*
Elizabeth Des Chenes, *Managing Editor*

LIBRARY OF CONGRESS CATALOGING-IN-PUBLICATION DATA

Epidemics / David Haugen and Susan Musser, book editors.
   p. cm. -- (Opposing viewpoints)
   Includes bibliographical references and index.
   ISBN 978-0-7377-5219-9 (hardcover) -- ISBN 978-0-7377-5220-5 (pbk.)
   1. Epidemics. 2. Epidemiology. I. Haugen, David M., 1969- II. Musser, Susan.
   RA653.E65 2011
   614.4--dc22
                         2010052249

Printed in the United States of America
1 2 3 4 5 6 7 15 14 13 12 11

Contents

Chapter 2: How Serious Was the Threat of an H1N1 Swine Flu Pandemic?

Chapter 3: Are Vaccines Harmful?

Chapter 4: Are America and the World Prepared for Coming Pandemics?

Why Consider Opposing Viewpoints?

> "The only way in which a human being can make some approach to knowing the whole of a subject is by hearing what can be said about it by persons of every variety of opinion and studying all modes in which it can be looked at by every character of mind. No wise man ever acquired his wisdom in any mode but this."
>
> John Stuart Mill

In our media-intensive culture it is not difficult to find differing opinions. Thousands of newspapers and magazines and dozens of radio and television talk shows resound with differing points of view. The difficulty lies in deciding which opinion to agree with and which "experts" seem the most credible. The more inundated we become with differing opinions and claims, the more essential it is to hone critical reading and thinking skills to evaluate these ideas. Opposing Viewpoints books address this problem directly by presenting stimulating debates that can be used to enhance and teach these skills. The varied opinions contained in each book examine many different aspects of a single issue. While examining these conveniently edited opposing views, readers can develop critical thinking skills such as the ability to compare and contrast authors' credibility, facts, argumentation styles, use of persuasive techniques, and other stylistic tools. In short, the Opposing Viewpoints Series is an ideal way to attain the higher-level thinking and reading skills so essential in a culture of diverse and contradictory opinions.

In addition to providing a tool for critical thinking, Opposing Viewpoints books challenge readers to question their own strongly held opinions and assumptions. Most people form their opinions on the basis of upbringing, peer pressure, and personal, cultural, or professional bias. By reading carefully balanced opposing views, readers must directly confront new ideas as well as the opinions of those with whom they disagree. This is not to simplistically argue that everyone who reads opposing views will—or should—change his or her opinion. Instead, the series enhances readers' understanding of their own views by encouraging confrontation with opposing ideas. Careful examination of others' views can lead to the readers' understanding of the logical inconsistencies in their own opinions, perspective on why they hold an opinion, and the consideration of the possibility that their opinion requires further evaluation.

Evaluating Other Opinions

To ensure that this type of examination occurs, Opposing Viewpoints books present all types of opinions. Prominent spokespeople on different sides of each issue as well as well-known professionals from many disciplines challenge the reader. An additional goal of the series is to provide a forum for other, less known, or even unpopular viewpoints. The opinion of an ordinary person who has had to make the decision to cut off life support from a terminally ill relative, for example, may be just as valuable and provide just as much insight as a medical ethicist's professional opinion. The editors have two additional purposes in including these less known views. One, the editors encourage readers to respect others' opinions—even when not enhanced by professional credibility. It is only by reading or listening to and objectively evaluating others' ideas that one can determine whether they are worthy of consideration. Two, the inclusion of such viewpoints encourages the important critical thinking skill of objectively evaluating an author's credentials and bias. This evaluation will illuminate an author's reasons for taking a particular stance on an issue and will aid in readers' evaluation of the author's ideas.

It is our hope that these books will give readers a deeper understanding of the issues debated and an appreciation of the complexity of even seemingly simple issues when good and honest people disagree. This awareness is particularly important in a democratic society such as ours in which people enter into public debate to determine the common good. Those with whom one disagrees should not be regarded as enemies but rather as people whose views deserve careful examination and may shed light on one's own.

Thomas Jefferson once said that "difference of opinion leads to inquiry, and inquiry to truth." Jefferson, a broadly educated man, argued that "if a nation expects to be ignorant and free . . . it expects what never was and never will be." As individuals and as a nation, it is imperative that we consider the opinions of others and examine them with skill and discernment. The Opposing Viewpoints Series is intended to help readers achieve this goal.

David L. Bender and Bruno Leone,
Founders

Introduction

"Mother Nature's potential threat may be, in the end, much greater than any destruction that could result from another world war, a nuclear bomb blast, or some heinous act of terrorism. In a worst-case scenario, the emergence of a new infectious disease with high transmissibility and mortality has the potential to devastate the human population before sufficient resources can be rallied effectively."

—Corrie Brown,
USA Today *magazine, May 2010*

"H1N1 [swine flu] makes clear how vulnerable our interconnected globe is to emerging diseases. As a result of jet travel and international trade, a new pathogen managed to seed itself in more than 20 countries in less than two weeks. But while globalization has its liabilities, it is also a strength because it gives us the tools to create a truly international disease-surveillance system."

—Bryan Walsh,
Time, *May 18, 2009*

Epidemics are common health concerns for local, regional, and even global medical authorities. Epidemics arise through various means—poor health or sanitation in populated areas, shifting human demographic patterns, changes in climate, or even the mutation of specific disease pathogens into new strains. Health authorities define epidemics as diseases that are more pervasive in a population than normally expected. Thus, if a seasonal influenza virus typically incapacitates seven thousand people in a large city, then an outbreak causing twelve thousand cases of illness could be termed an epidemic. For some diseases, such high numbers are not necessary to raise epidemic concerns. A rare contagious disease infecting fifty people, for example, might be deemed an epidemic if, in previously monitored periods, the population showed no signs of the illness. In the United States, the Centers for Disease Control and Prevention constantly revise the percentage of the population that must fall ill before declaring a disease an epidemic because new strains of specific pathogens come and go, altering the statistical rates of persons *expected* to become sick.

Epidemics differ from pandemics because the latter reflect global outbreaks of a disease. Writing in a December 19, 2003, article for *Slate*, columnist Brendan I. Koerner explains, "A pandemic is an epidemic that occurs across several countries and affects a sizable portion of the population in each, although there's no formal definition of what constitutes 'sizable.'" The World Health Organization (WHO) monitors influenza outbreaks and charts the spread of these pathogens through six degrees of global concern—from localized cases (stage 1) through pandemic (stage 6)—because various incarnations of this viral disease have often spread across the globe. In fact, the twentieth and twenty-first centuries have witnessed several deadly flu pandemics. The Spanish Flu (1918–1919) reached every continent and sickened roughly a third of the world's population (or about half a billion people). The most recent H1N1 swine flu pandemic of 2009 was reported to have infected more than thirty thousand people in seventy-four countries. The discrepancy seems great, but the WHO insists the 2009 swine flu qualified as a pandemic because it was not a recurring seasonal influenza (which typically claims more victims) and it arose in more individuals than WHO experts would expect a nonseasonal flu to infect. Other diseases such as the measles, typhus, and tuberculosis have also flared up into pandemics in recent history. Acquired immune deficiency syndrome (AIDS) has remained a virulent pandemic since it was first recognized in 1981. As a 2009 UNAIDS fact sheet reports, in 2008, there were between 31.1 million and 35.8 million people living with HIV (human immunodeficiency virus, the viral infection that leads to AIDS) in the world, between 2.4 million and 3.0 million new infections, and 1.7 million to 2.4 million deaths caused by AIDS or its resulting health problems.

The response to epidemics and pandemics is basically the same for both national and global health organizations. The first step is teaching prevention to curb the spread of diseases. Once a contagion begins spreading, though, health authorities continue to stress preventative measures while developing vaccines to create "herd immunity"—that is, a health care strategy based on the understanding that immunizing large numbers of people will slow the advance of a disease so that even unvaccinated individuals will be less likely to contract the illness. In some cases, the vaccines, when employed year after year, lead to the suppression of certain diseases. Smallpox, a disease that had plagued humankind for at least three thousand years, was completely eradicated following a global vaccination program in the 1960s. Slow transmission of the disease, rapid containment of infected individuals, and a vaccine that offered decade-long resistance proved a winning strategy against a virus that had caused 2 million deaths worldwide in 1967, the year the WHO launched its eradication program.

While the elimination of smallpox was a unique victory, some diseases have been able to overcome the health care measures meant to thwart them. Both the avian flu (H5N1) and the swine flu (H1N1) have produced vaccine-resistant strains. Some researchers fear that widespread inoculations might actually encourage the growth of these variants of the disease. In a July 29, 2009, article for LewRockwell.com, health writer Bill Sardi explains, "The paradox is that if the virulence of a vaccine-resistant flu strain is less than that of the vaccine-vulnerable strain, the epidemic might increase in proportion to the percentage of the population that elects to undergo vaccination." Similarly, many health authorities are warning people to refrain from overuse of antibiotics because some new, drug-resistant bacteria are evolving to defeat these common protections. Fox News reported on September 14, 2010, that "scientists have long feared this—a very adaptable gene that hitches onto many types of common germs and confers broad drug resistance, creating dangerous 'superbugs.'" With first-line defensive measures overcome, medical experts are scrambling to concoct remedies to deal with these new types of germs before they become epidemic or pandemic.

In *Opposing Viewpoints: Epidemics*, medical experts, health authorities, and journalists examine some of the common concerns about widespread diseases and their transmission. In the first two chapters, entitled, respectively, Do Epidemics Pose a Significant Health Risk? and How Serious Was the Threat of an H1N1 Swine Flu Pandemic?, these commentators debate the threat of contagious diseases and the potential for overreaction to pandemics. In the third chapter, Are Vaccines Harmful?, reporters and health professionals address the titular question and argue whether vaccination should be compulsory to safeguard public health. In the final chapter, Are America and the World Prepared for Coming Pandemics?, experts discuss the preparedness of America and the world to face emerging epidemics and pandemics as well as the threat of bioterrorism in the post-9/11 era. In all, the authors herein examine whether the world is focused enough on these health threats—scourges that have killed more citizens of the planet than any war or natural disaster—and whether the response, treatment, and potential cure for epidemic and pandemic diseases are safe and appropriate countermeasures. Confronting these challenges requires education, communication, transparency, and trust, and as the various arguments in this anthology point out, the world has not yet ensured its supply of these disease-fighters so that it can smoothly and efficiently combat the killer germs that still plague humanity.

Do Epidemics Pose a Significant Health Risk?

Chapter Preface

By September 2010, over eleven thousand cases of whooping cough (also known as pertussis) were reported across the United States for that year. Whooping cough is a bacterial disease that infects the lungs and causes a telltale cough that can last for weeks. The disease is easily spread and highly contagious. California alone recorded more than four thousand patients with the ailment, and nine infants in the state died from the disease between January and September. The Centers for Disease Control and Prevention states that such high numbers of infected individuals have not been seen since 1955. Speaking in a *USA Today* article from July 26, 2010, Gilberto Chavez, chief of the California Department of Public Health's Center for Infectious Disease, remarked, "This has the potential to become very huge, but we are at a point where we can contain it." California began issuing booster shots to new mothers after declaring the disease an epidemic in June, but despite Chavez's optimism, more than twenty-five hundred new cases appeared from July to September.

Outbreaks of whooping cough are common every two to five years, but the recent resurgence has been the most widespread and deadly in decades. Past outbreaks have always been contained relatively quickly, leaving most Americans unaware of the disease and its symptoms; however, like modern outbreaks of measles and other diseases the public thought conquered by science, whooping cough has only been kept at bay by routine childhood immunization. The DTaP (diphtheria, tetanus, and pertussis) vaccine administered in five doses before the age of seven is the preventive measure most regularly administered in the United States, but not all parents are convinced of the necessity and safety of this prophylactic. As Elizabeth Landau notes in a June 28, 2010, article for CNN.com, "Some doctors relate [the] recent rise in cases to the parents who have shied away from vaccinating children due to fears, albeit unfounded, that there is a connection between vaccines and autism." Landau goes on to claim that "a 2009 study in *Pediatrics* found that parental refusal of whooping cough vaccination was associated with children's risk of pertussis infection."

According to medical experts, lack of childhood vaccination coupled with waning immunization in adults is responsible for the reappearance of many epidemics not seen for decades in America. These outbreaks are a reminder that infectious diseases are still prevalent and lethal in the United States and across the globe. Virulent contagions never go away even if successful immunization programs erase them from memory. In the following chapter, various health professionals caution that modern science has not dispelled the health risks of certain contagions, even as other experts maintain that the global medical community can and has reduced the threat of pernicious disease epidemics.

| *"Emerging and re-emerging infections pose serious threats to the health of the American people."*

Infectious Diseases Are a Threat to America and the World

Margaret A. Hamburg et al.

In the following viewpoint, Margaret A. Hamburg and several colleagues, writing for the Trust for America's Health claim that emerging and existing diseases are a grave concern for America and the globe. In their view, many factors, such as poverty, deforestation, climate change, and globalization, have allowed diseases to evolve and spread rapidly in human communities. Though acknowledging the toll that disease has taken on populations across the world, Hamburg and her coauthors of the viewpoint focus on the impact on the United States. They assert that hundreds of thousands of Americans are infected with deadly and debilitating viruses each year, claiming lives and draining the economy. Hamburg and her colleagues maintain that the US government and the scientific community in the United States, as well as their counterparts abroad, must step up the

Margaret A. Hamburg et al., "Germs Go Global: Why Emerging Infectious Diseases Are a Threat to America," Trust for America's Health, October 2008. Reprinted by permission.

fight against this public health threat. A former senior scientist at the Nuclear Threat Initiative, Margaret A. Hamburg was confirmed in 2009 as the 21st commissioner of the US Food and Drug Association. Her associates on this viewpoint are members of the Trust For America's Health, a non-profit organization dedicated to preventative health.

As you read, consider the following questions:

1. What factors do Hamburg and her colleagues cite as contributors to the prevalence of drug-resistant microbes?

2. According to Hamburg's report, what is the most likely underlying reason for increased susceptibility to infectious diseases in children in America and across the globe?

3. According to a 2007 American Medical Association report cited by the authors, about how many Americas are infected with MRSA each year and how many die?

Emerging and re-emerging infectious diseases pose serious threats to the health of the American people. In 2003, the IOM [Institute of Medicine] issued *Microbial Threats to Health: Emergence, Detection, and Response*, an important follow up to the 1992 IOM report on emerging infectious diseases. The 2003 IOM report assessed the threats of emerging infectious diseases to the U.S. and warned:

"While dramatic advances in science and medicine have enabled us to make great strides in our struggle to prevent and control infectious diseases, we cannot fall prey to an illusory complacency ... Infectious diseases unknown in this country just a decade ago, such as West Nile encephalitis and hantavirus pulmonary syndrome, have emerged to kill hundreds of Americans—and the long-term consequences for survivors of the initial illnesses are as yet unknown. Other known diseases, including measles, multidrug-resistant tuberculosis, and even malaria, have been imported and transmitted within the United States in the last 10 years. . . . Compounding the threat posed by these infectious diseases is the continuing increase in antimicrobial resistance."

Diseases Becoming Drug Resistant

Antimicrobial resistance is a serious patient safety and public health issue. According to the National Institute of Allergy and Infectious Diseases (NIAID), "antimicrobial drug resistance is the ability of a microbe to grow in the presence of a chemical that would normally kill it or limit its growth." Disease-causing microbes that have become hard to treat with antibiotic drugs include *E. coli, Salmonella, Staphylococcus aureus,* and those causing TB [tuberculosis], gonorrhea, and malaria, among others. People infected with antimicrobial-resistant organisms are more likely to have longer hospital stays and may require more complicated treatment. . . .

Antimicrobial resistance is exacerbated by the overuse and misuse of antibiotics in people and animals, the lack of rapid diagnostic tests that can identify infectious agents, poor infection control in health care and community settings, and poor hand hygiene. The use of antibiotics in agriculture and aquaculture also contributes significantly to antimicrobial resistance. Preventing infection and decreasing inappropriate antibiotic use are important strategies for controlling resistance.

Globalization Spreads Disease

Globalization, the worldwide movement toward economic, financial, trade, and communications integration, has impacted public health significantly. Technology and economic interdependence allow diseases to spread globally at rapid speeds. Experts believe that the increase in international travel and commerce, including the increasingly global nature of food handling, processing, and sales contribute to the spread of emerging infectious diseases. Increased global trade has also brought more and more people into contact with zoonosis— diseases that originated in animals before jumping to humans. For example, in 2003, the monkeypox virus entered the U.S. through imported Gambian giant rats sold in the nation's under-regulated exotic pet trade. The rats infected pet prairie dogs, which passed the virus along to humans. International smuggling of birds, brought into the U.S. without undergoing inspection and/or quarantine, is of particular concern to public health experts who worry that it may be a pathway for the H5N1 "bird flu" virus to enter the country.

Lower cost and efficient means of international transportation allow people to travel to more remote places and potential exposure to more infections diseases. And the close proximity of passengers on passenger planes, trains, and cruise ships over the course of many hours puts people at risk for higher levels of exposure. If a person contracts a disease abroad, their symptoms may not emerge until they return home, having exposed others to the infection during their travels. In addition, planes and ships can themselves become breeding grounds for infectious diseases.

The 2002–2003 SARS [severe acute respiratory syndrome] outbreak spread quickly around the globe due to international travel. SARS is caused by a new strain of *coronavirus*, the same family of viruses that frequently cause the common cold. This contagious and sometimes fatal respiratory illness first appeared in China in November 2002. Within 6 weeks, SARS had spread worldwide, transmitted around the globe by unsuspecting travelers. According to CDC [Centers for Disease Control and Prevention], 8,098 people were infected and 774 died of the disease. . . .

Environmental Factors Aid Outbreaks

Geophysical phenomena such as shifts in temperature, wind, and rainfall patterns can precipitate the appearance of new diseases in new places. Weather and climate affect different diseases in different ways. For example, diseases transmitted by mosquitoes, such as dengue fever, Rift Valley fever, and yellow fever are associated with warm weather and experts believe that an El Niño occurrence (a fluctuation of the ocean-atmosphere system in the tropical Pacific having important consequences for weather around the globe), may be a factor in the resurgence of malaria and cholera. On the other hand, influenza becomes epidemic primarily during cool weather. Meningococcal meningitis is associated with dry environments, while cryptosporidiosis outbreaks are associated with heavy rainfall, which can overwhelm sewage treatment plants or cause lakes, rivers and streams to become contaminated by runoff which contains waste from infected animals.

Climate changes in North America are believed to be responsible for the growing populations of 2 new species of mosquitoes, including Asian tiger mosquitoes, in the continental U.S. These insects, which are believed to be successful bearers, or "vectors," of diseases like LaCrosse encephalitis, yellow fever, dengue fever, and West Nile virus, now infest more than 30 states. . . .

Deforestation and reforestation also can be factors in the spread and prevalence of certain emerging infectious diseases. Globally, rates of deforestation have grown significantly since the beginning of the 20th century. Driven by rapidly increasing human population numbers, large areas of tropical and temperate forests, as well as prairies, grasslands, and wetlands, have been converted to agricultural and ranching uses. The result has been an upsurge of certain infectious diseases, as the relationships between humans and disease vectors (carriers) shift. Deforestation, with subsequent changes in land use and human settlement patterns, has coincided with increased malaria prevalence in Africa, Asia, and Latin America. Conversely, reforestation in the Northeastern and the upper Midwest regions of the U.S. has promoted an increase in the population of the white-tailed deer, an important host for the ticks that carry Lyme disease.

Societal Factors

A number of societal factors contribute to the emergence and re-emergence of infectious disease. Poverty, lack of access to health care, poor sanitation, unsafe water, and a lack of proper hygiene all contribute to the expanding impact of infectious diseases.

Overcrowded and poor living conditions make people living in poverty especially vulnerable to communicable diseases such as TB and cholera. Limited access to health care and medicine can render otherwise treatable conditions such as malaria and TB fatal for those living in poverty. Urban decay and squalid living conditions and the presence of vermin also contribute to the spread of infections, such as plague. Meanwhile, contaminated water and inadequate sewage treatment systems in impoverished nations contribute to the spread of infectious diseases like cholera.

Poor nutrition and compromised immune systems are also key risk factors for several major diseases including lower respiratory infections, TB, and measles. There is increasing evidence that suggests that malnutrition is the underlying reason for increased susceptibility to infectious diseases especially in children. At the same time, infections, especially those associated with diarrhea, can lead to malnutrition in young children, so that diarrheal illness is both a cause and an effect of malnutrition.

War and civil strife generally result in a breakdown of domestic stability, food and water shortages, and destruction of the medical infrastructure, including existing vaccination programs. Refugee camps often are crowded and dirty, with little or no access to medical care or protection from disease transmission.

High-risk behaviors continue to be an important factor in the transmission of some infectious diseases. Sexual behavior and use of intravenous drugs continue to be primary modes of HIV [human immunodeficiency virus] transmission, and

Leading Infectious Causes of Death Worldwide

Cause	Rank	Estimated Number of Deaths
Respiratory infections	1	3,871,000
HIV/AIDS	2	2,866,000
Diarrheal diseases	3	2,001,000
Tuberculosis	4	1,644,000
Malaria	5	1,224,000
Measles	6	645,000
Pertussis	7	285,000
Tetanus	8	282,000
Meningitis	9	173,000
Syphilis	10	167,000

Note: Most recent World Health Organization statistics are from 2002. Rankings have remained unchanged since 1990.

TAKEN FROM: Margaret A. Hamburg et al., *Germs Go Global*, Washington, DC: Trust for America's Health, October 2008.

public health efforts over the last few decades have demonstrated how difficult such behaviors are to change. In developing nations, ignorance of preventive measures and the absence of social agencies to teach the avoidance of risky behaviors exacerbate the problem. Once diagnosed with a particular disease, failure to comply with prescribed treatment regimens is another factor of transmission. The emergence of drug-resistant TB can be attributed in large part to poor patient compliance with therapy.

Impact of Emerging Diseases

Emerging infectious diseases already pose a domestic health crisis.

West Nile virus is now endemic in the U.S. American troops are returning from Iraq and Afghanistan with highly drug resistant bacterial infections. Increasingly, locker rooms and gymnasiums are sources of staph infections. A heretofore unknown pathogen—SARS—emerged, causing illness, death, and economic mayhem. Public health officials remain on high alert for the first sign that the deadly H5N1 avian influenza virus has breached U.S. borders. An American citizen thought to have XDR-TB exposed the vulnerability of the U.S. public health system. Deadly foodborne disease outbreaks from domestic and imported agricultural products are increasingly commonplace. And, the U.S. has experienced its first deliberate and lethal attack using a biological agent as a weapon.

Emerging and re-emerging infectious diseases pose risks for all Americans. For example, if a severe infuenza outbreak were to occur, the U.S. government estimates that as many as 90 million Americans could become sick and 2 million might die. The consequences of a bioterror attack involving smallpox or anthrax are almost unfathomable.

While U.S. public health officials must be prepared for such scenarios, they remain hypothetical. There are, however, a number of emerging and re-emerging infections that are real threats to the health of Americans as well as the U.S. economy today.

High Prevalence and High Costs

There are 1.2 million people living with HIV/AIDS in the U.S., including more than 440,000 with AIDS [acquired immune deficiency syndrome]. There are an estimated 56,300 new cases of HIV diagnosed in this country every year. Nearly 566,000 Americans have died of AIDS since 1981. African Americans accounted for 49 percent of new HIV infections diagnosed in the U.S. in 2006, although they comprise only 13.8 percent of the population. The HIV infection rate among African Americans is 7 times higher than the rate among whites. The infection rate among Latinos is 3 times higher than the rate among whites.

As devastating as the health consequences of this infectious disease may be, the costs of treating HIV/AIDS are equally staggering. The annual per-patient medical expenses associated with doctor appointments, laboratory tests, and drugs to prevent or treat HIV-related opportunistic infections average from $18,000–$20,000, with even higher costs for those with more advanced HIV-related illness. These costs do not include those related to lost productivity.

The costs to the American taxpayer are also high. In Fiscal Year 2007, total federal spending on HIV/AIDS-related medical care, research, prevention, and other activities in the U.S. was $23.3 billion. Additionally, during the same time period, the share of state-Medicaid spending on AIDS was estimated to be $5.5 billion and states reported spending $294 million on their AIDS Drug Assistance Programs.

The MRSA [Methicillin-resistant *Staphylococcus aureus*] numbers are alarming too. A 2007 CDC-supported study published in the *Journal of the American Medical Association* estimated that MRSA infects more than 94,000 people and kills nearly 19,000 annually nationwide. That makes it the sixth leading cause of death in the U.S. MRSA-specific studies suggest that the additional cost of treating an antibiotic-resistant staph infection versus one that is not resistant range from a minimum of $3,000 to more than $35,000 per case. In 2005, such infections cost the health care system (patients and hospitals) an extra $830 million to $9.7 billion, before taking into account indirect costs related to patient pain, illness, and time spent in the hospital.

Hepatitis C is a liver disease caused by HCV [hepatitis C virus] and is transmitted through blood or other body fluids. These infections sometimes result in an acute illness, but most often become a chronic condition that can lead to cirrhosis of the liver and liver cancer.

In 2006, there were an estimated 19,000 new hepatitis C virus infections in the U.S. and an estimated 3.2 million Americans have chronic hepatitis C virus infection. Approximately 8,000–10,000 people die every year from hepatitis C related liver disease. It is the leading cause of cirrhosis and liver cancer and the most common reason for liver transplantation in the U.S.

According to the American Liver Foundation, medical expenditures for people with hepatitis C are estimated to be $15 billion annually. The projected direct and indirect costs of hepatitis C will be $85 billion for the years 2010–2019, as the number of people chronically infected will likely continue to increase.

Infections Making a Comeback

In addition to emerging infections, Americans also are increasingly at risk from re-emerging infectious diseases. For example, after seeing a decline in TB cases in the U.S. over the last decade, this contagious airborne disease could be on an upswing

Of particular concern is the number of cases of drug-resistant TB found in foreign-born individuals now residing in the U.S. According to a study conducted by CDC researchers, 57 percent of all TB cases in the U.S. were among foreign-born individuals in 2006. Approximately 10 percent of drug-resistant TB infections occurred among immigrants, refugees, and foreign visitors, compared with a little more than 4 percent of U.S.-born residents with active TB infection. . . .

Other infectious diseases, once thought to be under control, have experienced recent outbreaks in the U.S. They include pertussis (especially among adolescents), mumps, and measles, all of which are vaccine-preventable.

Food-Related Diseases on the Rise

Infectious diseases transmitted by foods have become a major public health concern in recent years. It seems that hardly a month goes by without the report of a foodborne illness outbreak in the U.S.

Approximately 76 million Americans—nearly one-quarter of the U.S. population—are sickened by foodborne disease each year. Of these, an estimated 325,000 are hospitalized and 5,000 die. Medical costs and lost productivity due to foodborne illnesses are estimated to cost $44 billion annually. Major outbreaks can also contribute to significant economic losses in the agriculture and food retail industries.

Several new foodborne pathogens have emerged over the last few decades. *E. coli* O157:H7 was first identified in 1982 during an outbreak of bloody diarrhea traced to hamburgers from a fast-food chain. *Cyclospora* emerged in 1992 as a foodborne pathogen, and was later traced to outbreaks in the U.S. from imported Guatemalan raspberries. In March 2008, melons imported from Honduras caused *Salmonella* infections in 16 states; and beginning in April 2008, a *Salmonella* outbreak, thought to be associated with jalapeño and Serrano peppers imported from Mexico, sickened at least 1,400 Americans in 43 states. In 2007, the U.S. Department of Agriculture issued 20 separate meat recalls due to potential *E. coli* contamination, and in February 2008, the department issued its largest beef recall in history—143 million pounds of beef—from a California meatpacking company.

The Need to Improve Prevention

Scientists worldwide—government and academic, together with their industry partners and international collaborators—have made great strides in understanding emerging and re-emerging infectious diseases. Many of these discoveries have resulted in novel diagnostics, anti-infective therapy, and vaccines. Yet, much remains to be done. The U.S. can, and should, improve and expand its diagnostic and disease surveillance capabilities, and dramatically increase its investment in developing new treatments and vaccines. Scientists also need to better understand mechanisms of drug resistance and develop new ways to circumvent this growing public health threat.

> *"Allowing the story [of an emergent disease] to go un-clarified leads . . . to a cultural atmosphere with a largely disproportionate fear of diseases which are, in reality, relatively under control."*

The Media Exaggerate the Risks of Infectious Diseases

Colin Schultz

Few would argue with the claim that newspaper journalism shapes public perceptions of emergent diseases; in the viewpoint that follows, Colin Schultz is concerned that, in too many instances, journalists often overdramatize the impact of diseases to make their stories more compelling. Schultz argues that this type of reporting distorts the risks associated with these diseases and unduly causes panic among readers. Schultz maintains that news reporters should strive to convey information without embellishing or skewing facts to provide sensational copy. Colin Schultz is a journalist from Ontario, Canada. His work can be found on several Canadian news websites and on the Daily Planet, a Discovery Channel project in Canada.

Colin Schultz, "From AIDS to SARS: The Media and Emergent Disease," *CMBR*, July 2010. Reprinted by permission.

As you read, consider the following questions:

1. Why does Schultz choose stories from the *New York Times* and Toronto *Globe and Mail* to make his argument?

2. Why does the author contend that the *New York Times* was needlessly sensationalizing when it reported in 1983 that AIDS had become the second leading cause of death among hemophiliacs?

3. According to Schultz, why is it worrisome that the criticisms leveled at the reporting of the AIDS crisis are similar to those leveled at the SARS outbreak?

Every reporting beat has that one event, or set of events, that thrusts it into the spotlight. The stories, regardless of what else is going on in the world, dominate the front page. For the political reporter, it's an election or a scandal. For the police beat, it's a serial killer or abducted child. For health reporters, the time when they are needed most, and when they need to perform their best, is during the onset of an emergent disease.

I aim to show that, for a number of reasons, major news outlets do a consistently poor job at these crucial times. The argument will cover three major fields: the reporting styles used, differing ideas of the role of the media, and how there seems to be a lack of learning from previous mistakes on a large scale.

The media under analysis in this paper are the [Toronto] *Globe and Mail* (henceforth, *Globe*), and the *New York Times* (henceforth, *Times*). These outlets were chosen because they are generally considered to be high quality newspapers. There is no sense basing an argument on the performance of a tabloid who aims at nothing more than sensationalism. The point being, if the flaws I will discuss appear in the 'better' newspapers, then it can be assumed the less rigorous outlets make similar mistakes.

The diseases under discussion are AIDS (acquired immune deficiency syndrome), which emerged around 1981, and SARS (sudden acute respiratory syndrome), which emerged in March 2003. The *Globe* and the *Times* were also selected because they represent the seat of where the diseases emerged most strongly. Despite the idea that San Francisco is most strongly associated with AIDS, New York City had the highest rate of the disease in the United States. The same is true in Canada with SARS and Toronto. The significance of this relationship is that the reporting being presented in these two locations directly relates to the health of the readers.

The analysis of journalistic style will be further broken down into three categories of decreasing severity.

Dramatic Language, Little Information

The first is the problem of language use. This problem is chiefly one of context. At the beginning of a new disease, the language used should be clear, free of jargon, and void of dramatics. While this could be said of journalism in general, it is of special significance at these times.

The following was published in the *Times* in 1983.

> Medical detectives are calling it the century's most virulent epidemic. It is as relentless as leukemia, as contagious as hepatitis, and its cause has eluded researchers for more than two years. Acquired immune deficiency syndrome, or AIDS, was first seen in homosexual men—particularly those who were promiscuous—but it has now struck so many different groups that its course cannot be predicted.
>
> ...The AIDS patient may survive his first bizarre infection, or his second, but he remains vulnerable to successive infections, one of which is likely to kill him.

The language used in this piece is clearly dramatic, and goes far beyond the purpose of alerting the public to a new threat. At this point, the population isn't informed, they're scared.

Another style of journalism which produces little more than fear is the feature. This is especially true of those with a softer style including scene setting, characters, etc. The purpose of using this style is to grab and hold the reader's attention.

One such simplification is the tendency to construct stories around individuals and personalities, rather than structures and social forces. While this personification might illustrate deep cultural ideals about individualism, it is also an attribute of storytelling whereby readers are drawn into the narrative through "identification" with another person [From the *Canadian Journal of Communication*].

One example of this stylistic technique gone wrong is in a *Times* piece on SARS, released within weeks of the initial outbreak.

On March 14, a worried father wheeled his adult son into the emergency room of Presbyterian Hospital here. The younger man was gasping for breath.

Ten minutes later, the nursing staff discovered that the young man went through Hong Kong recently. "He was a remarkably healthy-looking guy," said Pete Herendeen, a registered nurse who first examined the patient. "But he was acutely ill. Right away we had the sense that this might be an extraordinary case."

The problem with stories like this is they provide little new information, while exacerbating fear through the imagery used. This story specifically played off two conventional fears: a healthy person is being struck down during their prime, and a parent is unable to protect their child. These are very strong themes which would relate strongly to many readers, but they also work to over-dramatize the situation. . . .

Distorting Facts

A more serious infraction is because of bad science reporting. Misinterpreting numbers, the conclusion in a study, or having

Presenting the Rare, Novel, and Dramatic in Disease Coverage

The media function as a critical interface between the scientific community, government, and the public, with a responsibility to strike a careful balance between raising awareness of issues of public concern and irrationally alarming the public at large. Media coverage tends to be driven by issues that are rare, novel, and dramatic rather than those of higher relative risk. Viewers remember less than a quarter of the information and story topics in a typical newscast, and news media have shifted to a more personalized presentation that presents a risk as a direct threat to the viewer rather than generalized risk to a population. Since alarming content is more common in newscasts than reassuring or neutral content, and an estimated 11% of news articles include exaggerated claims, the possible impacts of disease being frequently presented in the media deserve attention.

Meredith E. Young, Geoffrey R. Norman,
and Karin R. Humphreys, PLoS ONE, *October 2008.*

an ill understanding of what makes a finding significant goes far beyond making the reader worried. It causes them to be misinformed.

In 1983, the *Times* ran an article with the title "Research Traces AIDS in 6 of 7 female partners." In the body of the work, however, it read,

> A study of seven female sexual partners of men with acquired immune deficiency syndrome, or AIDS, suggests that the disease may be sexually transmitted between heterosexual men and women, according to its authors.

Of the seven women in the study, which was reported in today's issue of *The New England Journal of Medicine*, one developed the disorder, another appeared to be in early stages of developing it, four had abnormalities linked to the syndrome and one was healthy.

The headline and text of the article are in conflict. One reported a 6 out of 7 relationship, and the other a 1 out of 7 ratio of confirmed cases. The headline greatly exaggerated the results of the study, giving the reader a distorted sense of risk.

Much later [in 2009], Candace Gibson wrote some advice [for Jsource, a Canadian journalism website] for how to cover emergent diseases.

As it took time for a reliable test for the SARS virus to be developed, cases were designated as 'suspect' until they could be confirmed or considered "probable" SARS. Reporting on the number of suspected cases greatly inflated the number of "real" cases of SARS and made the epidemic look much worse than it was.

This example represents how the misinterpretation of findings can skew a reader's understanding of the disease.

Inexperience Shows

Another way that AIDS was handled improperly is when journalists failed to accurately represent the numbers they used. In 1983 the *Times* ran an article where the reporter wrote, "[AIDS] has become the second leading cause of death among haemophiliacs." The article was accompanied by the headline "Disease Stirs Fear on Blood Supply". It wasn't revealed until much further down in the article that,

It has taken the lives of eight of the 70 haemophiliacs whose deaths were reported last year, Dr. Evatt said . . . [and] about 15,000 haemophiliacs live in the United States.

The actual severity of the issue, eight deaths out of a possible 15,000 who could have been afflicted, does not warrant the alarming headline. The finding that such a small percentage of the population of haemophiliacs developed AIDS, presumably from blood transfusions, is unlikely to be statistically significant. Further, it is irresponsible to assume the reader will get so far through the piece to finally get some context.

There is one other way that reporters misrepresented the science that I will discuss here. Sometimes, journalists will, in the attempt to find a new angle, report something prematurely. The *Globe* in 1986 ran the following lead,

> Scientists are not sure whether mothers can pass on the deadly AIDS virus through breast milk, and infected mothers in different parts of the world are consequently receiving conflicting advice on whether to breast-feed.

In the heart of the emergence of a new disease, the reporting of "maybes" is highly irresponsible. The readers need useful information, not hopes or unfounded worries.

These misrepresentations are serious, as they lead to a distorted understanding of the state of events. They could, however unfortunate it may be, be blamed on the complexity of the subject matter. In his analysis of the quality of AIDS coverage, James Kinsella wrote [in his 1992 book *Covering the Plague: AIDS and the American Media*],

> Science and medicine have been the stepchildren of news organizations, often covered by poorly trained, poorly educated reporters. In large part because of the lack of expertise, outbreaks of disease are treated haphazardly by the media.

There is no prerequisite for a health reporter to have a background in medicine, or even science in general. And so, these types of errors can be expected. . . .

Teaching Reporters How to Report on Diseases

The dissatisfaction with the media's ability to cover diseases is so strong that it has prompted external forces to intervene. In

2002, the International AIDS society established the Journalist-to-Journalist HIV/AIDS training program. In a [2008] report on the effectiveness of the program, they said,

> Journalists probably are the most able to efficiently disseminate pertinent information on a global scale and must do so in languages that are understood by the general public.

> By contrast, misinformation about HIV/AIDS might result in an increase in HIV transmission.

The HIV/AIDS training program is an example to highlight the third prong of the argument against the news media's ability to cover emergent diseases.

News organizations as a collective *have not* increased their ability to report on emergent diseases. The criticisms made about the reporting of AIDS are very similar to the criticisms of SARS coverage. [As Ivan Emke reported in a 2000 *Canadian Journal of Communication* article,] "One of the consistent critiques of the media coverage of AIDS is that the stories tended toward sensationalism". The same has been said about SARS, and most other diseases in the news. The simple fact that this paper could alternate so freely between examples from the SARS coverage and the AIDS coverage is a testament to how similar the reporting styles were. . . .

A Public Overestimation of Risks

The story of AIDS, or any other emergent disease, is likely to follow a certain pattern. People will over-estimate the risks when there are many unknowns. However, responsible news organizations must present the new information as it comes out. Especially the information that helps clear up the misinterpreted risk. [In a June 2001 article from the *New York Times*, John Tierney wrote,]

> "AIDS was a genuine crisis in the 1980's, but today it's no more a crisis than any other chronic disease suffered by

New Yorkers," said Dr. Elizabeth M. Whelan, the president of A.C.S.H. [American Council on Science and Health.] "We need to put AIDS in context and give it the proportionate share of resources. It shouldn't be getting more than its share because we've been brainwashed into thinking the numbers are greater than they are."

Allowing the story to go un-clarified leads to a persistent misunderstanding of the disease. And, if future emergent diseases are handled in the same way, it leads to a cultural atmosphere with a largely disproportionate fear of diseases which are, in reality, relatively under control.

The most effective role that the news media can play during the onset of an emergent disease is that of public informer. The story is already interesting enough that stylistic tricks are unnecessary to grab the reader's attention. The health information that people need to know, the things that will keep them healthy, should be passed along. Interpretations, conspiracy theories, and rumors will abound in the alternative media and social interactions. The responsible news media should combat this by being, above all else, the source of accurate and clear information.

"The [AIDS] pandemic continues to grow, gain force and destroy lives."

The AIDS Pandemic Is Still a Global Health Threat

Josh Ruxin

Josh Ruxin is the director of Rwanda Works, an organization that seeks to build poverty-elimination programs and foster prosperity in Rwanda. He has written extensively on the economic, social, and public health challenges Rwanda and other parts of Africa face. In the following viewpoint, Ruxin claims that the AIDS pandemic is still a serious global health threat. While many developed countries have implemented treatment plans to curtail the rapid spread of the disease within their own borders, Ruxin asserts that the disease is rampant in Africa, where drugs and preventative measures are not widespread. Ruxin blames inattentive or uncaring African governments for not allocating enough resources to educate the people about AIDS or to enact treatment programs. He also indicts US philanthropic health organizations for squandering AIDS funds meant for African relief and for not adopting a strategy that would conceive of the battle against AIDS as part of a broader global health initiative.

Josh Ruxin, "AIDS Is Still a Crisis. Is Anyone Really Surprised?" kristof.blogs.newyork times.com, May 2010. Reprinted by permission.

As you read, consider the following questions:

1. Of the 31 million HIV-positive people around the world, about how many living in low- and middle-income countries does Ruxin say are receiving drug treatment?

2. According to the author, how would universal condom use affect the AIDS epidemic?

3. In Ruxin's assessment, where do most of the dollars from taxpayer-supported, global AIDS initiatives go?

[S]cience and health reporter] Donald McNeil's recent [May 10, 2010,] reporting in *The New York Times* has abruptly reminded Americans of a reality that's already painfully clear to millions on the ground in Africa: current efforts to fight AIDS aren't good enough.

McNeil has drawn attention, in particular, to the thousands in Uganda who have tested H.I.V. positive and are then denied treatment. These individuals are at the back of an unfathomable queue, and they only move up into the ranks of those who receive anti-retrovirals when an opening is created by the death of someone already receiving treatment. It's heartbreaking, but shouldn't be at all surprising to those watching the global numbers and patterns.

The Pandemic Grows in Africa

The facts say it all: there are about 31 million H.I.V. positive people worldwide, with only about four million of them in low and middle income countries receiving drug treatment. The large majority of them, a staggering 22 million, live in Africa, and there, only about two to three million are on treatment. With approximately three million new infections every year and about two million deaths, the pandemic continues to grow, gain force and destroy lives.

While it has been well known for years that earlier treatment prolongs life, it was only in December 2009 that the World Health Organization altered its guidelines to be in step with wealthy countries. That shift has essentially broadened the field for those who should be on therapy today to roughly 14 million, a number that feels desperately out of reach given current resources and approaches. How can the global community possibly achieve this?

African Governments Not Invested

1) Countries themselves need to take charge and not be over-reliant on the international community. Uganda has seen its prosperity increase over recent years; it could easily extend its current partnerships with bilateral and multilateral organizations and provide funds out of its own coffers to expand treatment. However, like so many nations, it chooses not to do so. The government spends about $130 million—roughly 6% of its $2.5 billion annual budget—on AIDS programming—but upwards of 80 percent of that amount is donor-financed. This means that the government is spending about $20 million of its own money to fight AIDS. Not a very large chunk, all things considered.

Such paltry public health spending would be unacceptable in the industrialized world, even in a place with as paradoxical and frustrating a health care system as we have in the U.S. Uganda, Kenya, and so many other nations need not be held to a different standard, especially since treatment costs have fallen so dramatically.

2) Treatment alone is not going to make AIDS go away; prevention is cheaper and far more effective. Short of an effective vaccine, prevention efforts must be expanded dramatically. Few nations speak as openly and act as aggressively as Rwanda, where there is no wait list for drugs and where male circumcision is on the rise, as well as condom use. It's always been a central irony to the AIDS pandemic that if everyone

Impact of AIDS on Sub-Saharan Africa

Sub-Saharan Africa remains the region most heavily affected by HIV. In 2008, sub-Saharan Africa accounted for 67% of HIV infections worldwide, 68% of new HIV infections among adults and 91% of new HIV infections among children. The region also accounted for 72% of the world's AIDS-related deaths in 2008.

The epidemic continues to have an enormous impact on households, communities, businesses, public services and national economies in the region. In Swaziland, average life expectancy fell by half between 1990 and 2007, to 37 years. In 2008, more than 14.1 million [11.5 million–17.1 million] children in sub-Saharan Africa were estimated to have lost one or both parents to AIDS.

Women and girls continue to be affected disproportionately by HIV in sub-Saharan Africa. For example, in Côte d'Ivoire, home to the most serious epidemic in West Africa, HIV prevalence among females (6.4%) was more than twice as high as among males (2.9%) in 2005. In sub-Saharan Africa as a whole, women account for approximately 60% of estimated HIV infections.

Joint United Nations Programme on HIV/AIDS
and World Health Organization, December 2009.

started using condoms today, there would be no new cases of H.I.V. San Francisco essentially saw this happen in the days immediately after the pathogen had been identified but before drug therapy was widely available.

Sadly, many of the most vulnerable groups in the States and elsewhere are seeing new spikes in incidence, no doubt bred in part by complacency in the wake of effective therapies.

Without a vaccine in hand, it's past time to start heading in the direction of better prevention.

Spending Funds Wisely

3) Lastly, and perhaps most importantly, although much more funding is required for expansion of H.I.V. efforts, we need to take a close look at how efficiently current funds are deployed.

In many U.S.-supported initiatives that I've had the chance to observe, only a small percentage of our taxpayer dollars ever gets to the people who need the help the most. The vast majority is eaten up in studies, air tickets, consultants, reports, overhead, and profit, usually for U.S. firms. For years the Global Fund to Fight AIDS, Tuberculosis and Malaria has been discussed in the same breath as the US financing mechanism—PEPFAR (Presidential Emergency Plan for AIDS Relief). That conflation should end. The Global Fund puts countries themselves in the driver's seat. PEPFAR chooses its players—mainly D.C.-based contractors—and its rate of government collaboration varies dramatically. U.S. dollars should build capacity in other nations to take over these programs, not cultivate a legacy of dependency.

The Global Fund and PEPFAR should be looking to strengthen the entire health system in poor countries, not merely those pieces that directly address HIV/AIDS. One of the broadest steps that global players must take is to stop viewing AIDS through a narrow lens and relegating it to its own area of public health. AIDS patients don't exist in a vacuum, yet I've seen elaborate structures built with our money for AIDS-specific services. Instead, AIDS programs should be fully integrated into the health system alongside malaria, maternal services, and primary health care.

While some countries such as Rwanda have been savvy and strategic about using the foundation of these funds to do just that, the vast majority have not, due to a lack of management resources and structured thinking (not to mention government commitment). It's time to get serious about the short-falls and the opportunities. We owe at least that to the 7,000 who perish daily from a pandemic that we can overcome.

| *"There is a way to completely wipe [AIDS] out—at least in theory."*

The AIDS Pandemic Can Be Eliminated

Clare Wilson

In the following viewpoint, Clare Wilson, the medical features editor for New Scientist *magazine, reports that several health officials working on the spread of human immunodeficiency virus (HIV) and its resultant acquired immune deficiency syndrome (AIDS) are suggesting that universal testing of at-risk populations may be the key to stopping this pandemic. As Wilson writes, new drug combinations have been successful in reducing the rate of infection among HIV carriers, and doctors and scientists believe that if individuals who are HIV positive receive drug treatment early enough, they will not likely pass on the disease. Thus, as Wilson explains, health officials anticipate that if governments implemented universal testing among at-risk populations, the disease could be eliminated. Wilson also reports, however, that obstacles to universal testing include its cost and its potential intrusion on civil liberties.*

Clare Wilson, "How to Eradicate AIDS," *New Scientist*, February 21, 2009. Reproduced by permission.

As you read, consider the following questions:

1. According to Wilson, what is the CD4 threshold for starting drug therapy in most wealthy nations today?

2. The author writes that in 2008, the United Kingdom's Health Protection Agency endorsed guidelines that would require people of what ages to take routine HIV tests when they entered a hospital or signed on with a primary care physician?

3. As Wilson reports, why does Kevin De Cock believe that investing $3.5 billion per year in making a country like Malawi nearly HIV free is better than investing less money in funding drug treatments?

What if we could rid the world of AIDS? The notion might sound like fantasy: HIV infection has no cure and no vaccine, after all. Yet there is a way to completely wipe it out—at least in theory. What's more, it would take only existing medical technology to do the job.

Here's how it works. If someone who is HIV positive takes antiretroviral-drug therapy they can live a long life and almost never pass on the virus, even through unprotected sex. So if everyone with HIV were on therapy, there would be little or no transmission. Once all these people had died, of whatever cause, the virus would be gone for good.

It's a simple idea, but the obstacles to implementing it worldwide are enormous. Persuading everyone with HIV to start therapy purely for public health reasons could be ethically dubious. To identify everyone who is HIV positive would require such widespread testing that some may feel it breached their civil liberties. Then there is the question of who would fund such a massive undertaking.

Yet the idea of eliminating HIV is so appealing, and the benefit to humanity so huge, that scientists and policy-makers are seriously considering the concept, albeit on regional scales.

In the next few months the World Health Organization (WHO) will meet to discuss how the idea could be tried in developing countries, and something approaching eradication might be attempted in the UK within the next decade. "You could eliminate transmission overnight," says Marcus Conant, an HIV specialist in San Francisco.

Better Treatment, Longer Lives

A plan like this can only be countenanced thanks to some sweeping changes over the past decade in the way HIV is managed by doctors and viewed by the public. In 1985, when HIV testing began, no treatment for the virus existed, so a positive result was effectively a death sentence. Fear of the virus and the fact that it spread most easily among gay men and intravenous drug users meant people with HIV were shunned, as well as being barred from taking out health and life insurance. The decision to have the test was generally an agonising one and many decided it was better not to know.

It was not until the mid-1990s and the arrival of cocktails of antiviral drugs that people with HIV could begin to imagine surviving for any significant length of time. Fear of the virus subsided and public attitudes began to soften. The beauty of these cocktails lies in the combination of drugs. If just one drug is taken, HIV can mutate and become resistant to it, but with three drugs the virus would need three simultaneous mutations to become resistant, a highly improbable event. This "triple therapy" stops viral replication in its tracks and seems to hold AIDS at bay indefinitely. People now had every reason to take the test.

If treatment for the virus has changed dramatically, so too has treatment timing. HIV progression is gauged by measuring levels of CD4 cells—immune cells that the virus infects and kills. A typical healthy person has more than 500 of these cells per microlitre of blood, while someone with HIV sees their count gradually fall. Once their CD4 count falls below about 200, the immune system can no longer fight off common pathogens, leading to "opportunistic" infections such as pneumonia and thrush.

Starting Antiretroviral Therapy Earlier

In the early days, doctors tended to delay triple therapy until a patient's CD4 count had dropped to about 200, on the basis that this would catch most people before opportunistic infections struck. There were good reasons not to start treatment sooner: the first antiretrovirals had nasty side effects and involved taking up to 20 tablets a day. What's more, at a time when only a few antiretrovirals existed, it was a real concern that if drug resistance developed, an individual could run out of medicines to take. Today, these obstacles have largely disappeared: people on the latest regimens take only one or two pills a day with few side effects, if any, and there are two dozen drugs to choose from.

We know now that starting treatment earlier than at a CD4 count of 200 brings health benefits. As well as reducing the risk of opportunistic infections, a large study showed [in 2008] that people who began treatment with a CD4 count above 350 are less likely to develop conditions usually seen as unrelated to HIV, such as heart or kidney disease. Researchers now suspect that long-term HIV infection causes a low-level activation of the immune system that can damage the heart, kidneys and liver. For these reasons, the treatment threshold in wealthy nations is now 350.

Of course this can only happen if someone has been diagnosed, something that often happens dangerously late. In the west, about one-quarter of people with HIV only discover their status when they are admitted to hospital with an opportunistic infection or cancer. Some die before triple therapy can take effect—from pneumonia, for example.

Widespread Testing

It is the benefits of early treatment, combined with the perils of late diagnosis, that have convinced many doctors and patient groups to urge that HIV tests be used more widely. For example, [in 2008] the UK government's Health Protection Agency [HPA] endorsed guidelines saying that in urban areas of the UK where people with undiagnosed infections are likely to be concentrated, HIV tests should be more widely available. In these places, everyone from 15 to 60 should have the test routinely when they register with a primary care doctor or are admitted to hospital. "We want normalisation of testing," says Barry Evans, an epidemiologist at the HPA. "They should get tested like they get their blood pressure checked."

Earlier HIV diagnosis not only helps the infected person, it also benefits everyone else. Once someone knows they are HIV positive, they are less likely to pass the virus to others through unsafe sex or sharing needles. The really important factor, though, is that therapy stops viral replication, so that much less virus reaches an infected person's bodily fluids.

Just how much this reduces the risk of transmission is a matter of great debate. Most of the evidence comes from studies of monogamous heterosexual couples who are "serodiscordant"—in other words one person is HIV positive and the other is not. Some studies have found a transmission rate of zero, but only in people who scrupulously take their tablets, so that no virus is detectable in their blood, and who are free of other sexually transmitted infections.

Early Treatment

[In 2008], a group of HIV specialists on the Swiss government's AIDS commission (EKAF) announced that HIV-positive people who met these conditions were "sexually non-infectious". For the first time serodiscordant heterosexual couples got official approval to bin [throw out] their condoms. Other experts disagree with the Swiss decision, pointing out that the virus can sometimes be found in semen and vaginal fluid even if it is undetectable in blood. Also, as the research results come from straight couples, it is unclear how the advice applies to gay men. Despite these doubts, some doctors now see patients with normal CD4 counts asking to start therapy purely to avoid passing on the virus.

While it is debatable just how small the transmission risk really is, it is indisputably much lower for patients taking antiretroviral therapy than for those who are not. That has led researchers to start speculating about expanding testing and treatment to everyone with HIV. In November 2008, a paper published in *The Lancet*, written by five of the WHO's leading AIDS specialists, drew the widest attention so far.

The researchers looked at the case for eradication in South Africa, which has the highest number of HIV cases in the world. They modelled what would happen if everyone over 15 were given annual tests, with all those who tested positive offered free antiretroviral treatment immediately, regardless of their CD4 count. They plugged in actual figures from a free treatment programme in Malawi to factor in people who decline therapy, stop because of side effects or switch drugs because of resistance.

The team found that within 10 years, the scheme would slash new HIV infections from the 1 in 50 people at present to less than 1 in 1000. Within 50 years, as people with HIV died (mainly from other causes), prevalence in the general population would fall from about 10 per cent to less than 1 per cent.

Screening and Treatment

That all sounds great, but the cost of the scheme would initially be about $3.5 billion a year. That might sound prohibitive, but the key comparison to make is with the cost of alternative plans. Today, aid programmes can fund antiretroviral treatment for only about one-third of people in the developing world with a CD4 count below 200. All the major HIV organisations, such as UNAIDS and the WHO, and several western governments including the UK's, are now calling for universal access to therapy, by which they mean getting the drugs to everyone with a count below 200. Some want the threshold to be raised to 350 in the developing world too.

However, the problem with this form of universal access is that it would do little to curb transmission, because everyone with CD4 counts above the threshold would still be spreading the virus. The cost of such a scheme would almost certainly rise over time as more people became infected, unlike the WHO experts' more ambitious scheme. "The [elimination] strategy becomes cost-saving in the future, despite initially increased costs," says Kevin De Cock, director of the WHO's HIV/AIDS department and one of the paper's authors. By 2030 it would become cheaper than using a 350 threshold.

The idea is still very much in its early stages, with De Cock stressing they are "not suggesting a change in policy but stimulating a discussion". In the next few months [of the first half of 2009], the WHO will bring together scientists, policymakers and funders to discuss employing the strategy in developing countries.

In some ways it might be easier to attempt universal treatment in a developed country. For example, the UK could, if it chose, afford to put every one of its estimated 73,000 HIV-positive residents on antiretroviral therapy. On the other hand, with HIV only affecting 0.1 per cent of the UK population, universal testing would be hard to justify. The modelling from *The Lancet* paper would have to be redone for the UK, where, unlike in South Africa, transmission is primarily among gay men. (Cases among heterosexuals are rising; these are mainly immigrants who have caught the virus abroad.) "We're trying to focus more on certain population groups or areas," says Tim Chadborn of the HPA.

Conant, however, argues that testing everyone would help to further reduce the stigma around AIDS. HIV may no longer be an automatic bar for health insurance but there is still an image problem for a disease that in the west is still seen as affecting mainly gay men, immigrants, prostitutes and drug addicts. Conant advocates mass testing in the US at churches and meetings of professional groups such as doctors—as happens today at gay bars. "It has got to be universal," he says.

Perhaps the most medically contentious part of the eradication plan, in any country, is that all those diagnosed positive would begin antiretroviral treatment immediately. At present there is no firm evidence that HIV does any damage to an individual as long as their CD4 count is above 350. "There are great big ethical problems about recommending treatment to someone when it's not clinically beneficial to that person," says Chadbourn.

A Test Program Begins

Still, no one really knows what the effects of starting treatment earlier are. This question should be answered by a large international trial called START, organised by the US National Institutes of Health, to compare the health of people who start therapy at 350 with that of people who start at over 500. The results will not be in for six years [until 2015], though.

If the people in the over-500 group do best, the main medical objection to eradication disappears. "If we can establish that there's a benefit, I would imagine that we would try to do exactly what's being proposed in *The Lancet* paper," says Andrew Phillips, an epidemiologist at the Royal Free and University College Medical School in London who is involved in START.

If a western country introduces widespread testing and immediate treatment, new infections should dwindle. "If there are benefits for the individual and benefits for the population, I would very strongly support that," says Evans. He would contemplate eradication even if the over-500 group in the START trial does no better than the 350 group, as long as it does no worse.

Perhaps the biggest obstacle would be the importation of HIV from abroad. The HPA now recommends that migrants from countries with high HIV rates be offered a test when they access any health service, such as registering with a primary care doctor. The agency frowns on testing at ports of entry in case it encourages discrimination.

Obstacles to Universal Implementation

Residents also import HIV by having unsafe sex while abroad. People would have to be persuaded to take the test when they returned. For Brian Gazzard, one of the UK's leading HIV specialists, based at the Chelsea and Westminster Hospital in London, this makes eradication on a country-by-country basis unfeasible. "It's got to be done worldwide," he says. "A public debate about that issue would be wonderful."

Western countries without state-funded healthcare would hit bigger problems. In the US, for example, many people with HIV delay starting therapy because they pay part or all of the cost. "The government would have to pay," says Conant.

Treatment standards would also have to improve in the US. Some health insurers insist that patients see primary care doctors rather than more expensive specialists. According to Conant, some non-specialists fail to use drug regimens that totally block viral replication, so the virus can still be transmitted. "That's the most common mistake I see," he says.

There are many obstacles to be overcome if any form of eradication plan, national or global, is to be attempted. Yet the damage done by AIDS is so huge that the chance to rid just some places of it has to be worth considering.

What is certain is that, however and wherever it is attempted, such a scheme will be controversial. Hard-line religious groups that view AIDS as divine retribution are unlikely to help out. Some liberals, on the other hand, might resist the idea of mass testing. "Should we try a social intervention which infringes on people's civil liberties?" asks Conant. "AIDS infringes upon people too. If we're going to stop this epidemic, this is a responsibility that society has to shoulder."

| "The threat of a global heterosexual
[AIDS] pandemic has disappeared."

The Threat of a Heterosexual AIDS Pandemic Is Over

Jeremy Laurance

Kevin De Cock, a Belgian-born scientist who is now the HIV/ AIDS director at the World Health Organization, made a bold statement in 2008 that the spread of human immunodeficiency virus (HIV) and its resultant acquired immune deficiency syndrome (AIDS) has never been a serious threat to heterosexual populations outside sub-Saharan Africa. In the following viewpoint, Jeremy Laurance, the health editor for the Independent newspaper in the United Kingdom, reports De Cock's claims. According to De Cock, HIV and AIDS have largely been confined to high-risk populations—such as sex workers and men who have sex with men—and have not penetrated very far into heterosexual populations. While De Cock acknowledges that this may mean that some AIDS funds have been misspent educating relatively safe communities, he contends that the spread of information is helpful in reminding people that the disease is still a

Jeremy Laurance, "Threat of World Aids Pandemic among Heterosexuals Is Over, Report Admits," *Independent* (UK), June 2008. Reprinted by permission.

pandemic. He believes more efforts need to be focused on Africa's AIDS plight and any surges in the disease among high-risk groups around the world.

As you read, consider the following questions:

1. Besides sex workers and men having sex with men, what other high-risk group does Laurance say is still threatened by HIV/AIDS infection?

2. According to the author, by what percentage does circumcision reportedly cut the rate of HIV infection?

3. What sub-Saharan country has witnessed the worst rates of infection, according to Laurance's report?

A quarter of a century after the outbreak of Aids, the World Health Organisation (WHO) has accepted that the threat of a global heterosexual pandemic has disappeared.

In the first official admission that the universal prevention strategy promoted by the major Aids organisations may have been misdirected, Kevin De Cock, the head of the WHO's department of HIV/Aids said there will be no generalised epidemic of Aids in the heterosexual population outside Africa.

Confined Primarily to High-Risk Groups

Dr De Cock, an epidemiologist who has spent much of his career leading the battle against the disease, said understanding of the threat posed by the virus had changed. Whereas once it was seen as a risk to populations everywhere, it was now recognised that, outside sub-Saharan Africa, it was confined to high-risk groups including men who have sex with men, injecting drug users, and sex workers and their clients.

Dr De Cock said: "It is very unlikely there will be a heterosexual epidemic in other countries. Ten years ago a lot of people were saying there would be a generalised epidemic in Asia—China was the big worry with its huge population. That

> ## Scaremongering and Gross Exaggerations
>
> The AIDS pandemic has ... passed its peak ... [and] many commentators now acknowledge the gross exaggerations and scaremongering of the AIDS bureaucracy. It is clear that HIV has remained largely confined to people following recognised high-risk behaviours, rather than being, in the mantra of the AIDS bureaucracy, a condition of poverty, gender inequality and under-development.
>
> *Michael Fitzpatrick, Spiked, August 2008.*
> *www.spiked-online.com.*

doesn't look likely. But we have to be careful. As an epidemiologist it is better to describe what we can measure. There could be small outbreaks in some areas."

In 2006, the Global Fund for HIV, Malaria and Tuberculosis, which provides 20 per cent of all funding for Aids, warned that Russia was on the cusp of a catastrophe. An estimated 1 per cent of the population was infected, mainly through injecting drug use, the same level of infection as in South Africa in 1991 where the prevalence of the infection has since risen to 25 per cent.

Dr De Cock said: "I think it is unlikely there will be extensive heterosexual spread in Russia. But clearly there will be some spread."

Inaccurate Estimations Cause Controversy

Aids still kills more adults than all wars and conflicts combined, and is vastly bigger than current efforts to address it. A joint WHO/UN Aids report published [in June 2008] showed that nearly three million people are now receiving antiretroviral drugs in the developing world, but this is less than a third of the estimated 9.7 million people who need them. In all there were 33 million people living with HIV in 2007, 2.5 million people became newly infected and 2.1 million died of Aids.

Aids organisations, including the WHO, UN Aids and the Global Fund, have come under attack for inflating estimates of the number of people infected, diverting funds from other health needs such as malaria, spending it on the wrong measures such as abstinence programmes rather than condoms, and failing to build up health systems.

Dr De Cock labelled these the "four malignant arguments" undermining support for the global campaign against Aids, which still faced formidable challenges, despite the receding threat of a generalised epidemic beyond Africa.

Any revision of the threat was liable to be seized on by those who rejected HIV as the cause of the disease, or who used the disease as a weapon to stigmatise high risk groups, he said.

"Aids still remains the leading infectious disease challenge in public health. It is an acute infection but a chronic disease. It is for the very, very long haul. People are backing off, saying it is taking care of itself. It is not."

The Danger of Neglect

Critics of the global Aids strategy complain that vast sums are being spent educating people about the disease who are not at risk, when a far bigger impact could be achieved by targeting high-risk groups and focusing on interventions known to work, such as circumcision, which cuts the risk of infection by 60 per cent, and reducing the number of sexual partners.

There were "elements of truth" in the criticism, Dr De Cock said. "You will not do much about Aids in London by spending the funds in schools. You need to go where transmission is occurring. It is true that countries have not always been good at that."

But he rejected an argument put in *The New York Times* that only $30m (£15m) had been spent on safe water projects, far less than on Aids, despite knowledge of the risks that contaminated water pose.

"It sounds a good argument. But where is the scandal? That less than a third of Aids patients are being treated—or that we have never resolved the safe water scandal?"

One of the danger areas for the Aids strategy was among men who had sex with men. He said: "We face a bit of a crisis [in this area]. In the industrialised world transmission of HIV among men who have sex with men is not declining and in some places has increased.

"In the developing world, it has been neglected. We have only recently started looking for it and when we look, we find it. And when we examine HIV rates we find they are high.

"It is astonishing how badly we have done with men who have sex with men. It is something that is going to have to be discussed much more rigorously."

Sub-Saharan Africa's Risk Factors

The biggest puzzle was what had caused heterosexual spread of the disease in sub-Saharan Africa—with infection rates exceeding 40 per cent of adults in Swaziland, the worst-affected country—but nowhere else.

"It is the question we are asked most often—why is the situation so bad in sub-Saharan Africa? It is a combination of factors—more commercial sex workers, more ulcerative sexually transmitted diseases, a young population and concurrent sexual partnerships."

"Sexual behaviour is obviously important but it doesn't seem to explain [all] the differences between populations. Even if the total number of sexual partners [in sub-Saharan Africa] is no greater than in the UK, there seems to be a higher frequency of overlapping sexual partnerships creating sexual networks that, from an epidemiological point of view, are more efficient at spreading infection."

Low rates of circumcision, which is protective, and high rates of genital herpes, which causes ulcers on the genitals through which the virus can enter the body, also contributed to Africa's heterosexual epidemic.

But the factors driving HIV were still not fully understood, he said.

"The impact of HIV is so heterogeneous. In the US, the rate of infection among men in Washington DC is well over 100 times higher than in North Dakota, the region with the lowest rate. That is in one country. How do you explain such differences?"

> *"Over the last decade, mean body mass index (BMI) has increased in virtually all Western European countries, Australia, New Zealand, Mexico, the United States, and China."*

The Obesity Epidemic Poses a Global Health Threat

Rita E. Carey

In the following viewpoint, Rita E. Carey asserts that people around the world are gaining too much weight, leading her and medical colleagues to insist that obesity has become an epidemic. According to Carey, the cheap price and widespread availability of energy-dense foodstuffs is the chief culprit of global weight gain. She maintains, however, that less exercise, the ease of modern lifestyles, and too many inert activities—such as television viewing—ensure that the high-calorie food is turned quickly into fat. Carey advocates for changes in public policy that will encourage more physical activity and educate people to make better dietary choices. Rita E. Carey is a clinical dietician and diabetes educator in Arizona.

Rita E. Carey, "The Obesity Epidemic: It's Not a Small World After All," *Today's Dietitian*, October 2006, p. 24. Reprinted by permission.

As you read, consider the following questions:

1. According to Carey's research, what percentage of American children between the ages of six and nineteen are now considered obese?

2. What are some of the examples the author gives of high-calorie-corn-added foods?

3. How does socioeconomic status influence obesity statistics, according to Carey?

We have all heard the statistics: An estimated 65% of Americans are overweight or obese and the current course of communal weight gain shows no sign of abating. Equally disturbing is the fact that people around the world are getting heavier as many European and other nations follow a similar pattern of "growth." Theories abound as to why this trend is occurring. These include, but are clearly not limited to, reduced physical activity, increased consumption of energy-dense meals and snacks, food insecurity, and the loss of traditional, cultural rituals linked with food. Many studies and surveys have been conducted to determine how to reverse this global epidemic, and the data offer at least some insight into the ways both human lifestyles and bodies are changing worldwide.

Obesity Becoming the Norm

The increased prevalence of individuals who are overweight and obese in the United States and Europe, as well as South America and Asia, has made thinning, or even stable weight, populations the exception rather than the norm. Though the United States leads the pack in the rate of weight gain over the longest period of time, Spain, Portugal, Ireland, Greece, Great Britain, Italy, Poland, Finland, and, yes, even France are showing a similar, if slower, trend. In fact, over the last decade, mean body mass index (BMI) has increased in virtually all Western European countries, Australia, New Zealand, Mexico, the United States, and China while decreasing weight trends have been mostly limited to some Eastern European states. Much of the increased prevalence of overweight and obesity throughout the world has been noted in children and adolescents—a disturbing trend, since many overweight adolescents become obese adults.

The prevalence of overweight and obesity in U.S. children and adolescents has tripled in the last three decades and research indicates that 15% of Americans between the ages of 6 and 19 are now obese. By comparison, in England, from 1980 through 2002, obesity in youths aged 6 to 15 increased to 16% of the population. Children are growing heavier at a slower rate in France, where the prevalence of overweight in 2000 was similar to that recorded in the United States in the late 1980s, and the incidence of obesity was similar to U.S. rates in the late 1970s.

However, the numbers of overweight children may vary greatly from region to region in France and other countries as well. For example, 17% of children in Roubaix, an economically depressed industrial town in northern France, are obese. In this region, 51% of the population is overweight or obese (compared with the 2003 national average of 42%) and the prevalence of obesity is increasing most rapidly in children and adolescents.

The average incidence of obesity in European adults is between 10% and 25% for both genders and has increased, depending on location, up to 40% over the last few decades. In England, for example, obesity in adult women rose to 23% and obesity in adult men nearly quadrupled to 22% from 1980 to 2002. By comparison, in the United States, 64% of adults aged 20 or older were classified as overweight and 30% were considered obese in 2000, a rise of more than 60% in some age groups since 1990.

2009 State Obesity Rates

State	%	State	%	State	%	State	%
Alabama	31.0	Illinois	26.5	Montana	23.2	Rhode Island	24.6
Alaska	24.8	Indiana	29.5	Nebraska	27.2	South Carolina	29.4
Arizona	25.5	Iowa	27.9	Nevada	25.8	South Dakota	29.6
Arkansas	30.5	Kansas	28.1	New Hampshire	25.7	Tennessee	32.3
California	24.8	Kentucky	31.5	New Jersey	23.3	Texas	28.7
Colorado	18.6	Louisiana	33.0	New Mexico	25.1	Utah	23.5
Connecticut	20.6	Maine	25.8	New York	24.2	Vermont	22.8
Delaware	27.0	Maryland	26.2	North Carolina	29.3	Virginia	25.0
Washington, DC	19.7	Massachusetts	21.4	North Dakota	27.9	Washington	26.4
Florida	25.2	Michigan	29.6	Ohio	28.8	West Virginia	31.1
Georgia	27.2	Minnesota	24.6	Oklahoma	31.4	Wisconsin	28.7
Hawaii	22.3	Mississippi	34.4	Oregon	23.0	Wyoming	24.6
Idaho	24.5	Missouri	30.0	Pennsylvania	27.4		

TAKEN FROM: Centers for Diseases Control and Prevention, *US Obesity Trends: Trends by State 1985–2009*, July 27, 2010. www.cdc.gov.

Obesogenic Conditions

Quite a bit of research has been conducted to determine precisely why this worldwide increase in human girth has occurred. Clearly, no single factor is responsible; it is the prevalence and spread of a variety of "obesogenic" conditions in both developed and developing nations that lies at the root of the problem. This term consolidates the changes in food availability and type, cultural rituals and attitudes, transportation modes, community size and shape, socioeconomic status, physical activity levels, and related shifts in lifestyle and diet that promote weight gain in a given population over time. When all the real and potential factors are considered together, it becomes apparent that, just as no single factor is responsible for this problem, no single factor can "solve" it.

Too Many Calories

Surplus food energy contributes to the obesity epidemic in the United States and abroad. Since the 1970s, America's average daily intake of calories has increased by 10%, or approximately 200 calories. Concurrently, per capita availability of sweeteners and fats increased by 20%. In fact, statistically, every American has access to nearly 4,000 calories per day, if all available food energy were divided evenly among us all. A large portion of these extra calories likely originates from the massive surplus of corn that has been produced in the farm belt since farm subsidy programs were changed in the late 1970s.

This fact may seem confusing at first—obviously, Americans and others are not gaining weight by directly eating more corn. They may, however, be packing on the pounds by eating it indirectly, in large quantities, in the form of inexpensive sweeteners, beverages, snacks, fast foods, and meat (a large amount of corn is utilized as animal feed). Because a huge surplus of corn is produced annually, it has become an inexpensive resource that can be converted into a wide variety of foods that pack a lot of calories for a small price. Americans, though they try, cannot possibly consume all the calories available from corn and its by-products, so many calories are exported to European countries, again in the form of beverages, snacks, and fast foods.

In fact, a recent study by the World Health Organization found that increased BMI in virtually all Western European countries, Australia, the United States, and China was positively correlated with the availability of surplus calories. This study did not ascertain what foods provided the surplus calories, but market trends in Europe indicate significant growth in fast food and beverage markets over the same time period.

An overabundance of food and calories combined with major international and domestic corporations' desire to exhibit continued financial growth creates a barrage of campaigns designed to convince people to eat more than they physically need. Strategies to encourage people to eat more food include creating foods that are convenient to prepare and eat on-the-go, making such foods available everywhere at low costs (including schools and workplaces), advertising, increasing variety and thus encouraging the "buffet syndrome," and providing larger portions for minimal additional cost. All these strategies are employed in countries around the world and they appear to be having an effect on when, why, and how much people eat.

Poverty and Energy-Dense Foods

Extra calories in the market are usually sold as energy-dense foods—ie, items packing a lot of calories into small, shelf-stable packages. The increased availability of these foods clearly promotes weight gain, especially in lower-income populations, though the reason for this may not be readily apparent.

Individuals faced with poor incomes will likely purchase foods that provide sufficient calories and satiety at a lower cost (caloric deficiencies usually occur only with overt food scarcity). Energy-dense foods are often less expensive (in dollars per calorie) than energy-dilute options and represent a large percentage of the diets of economically disadvantaged people.

Energy-dilute foods—such as fruits, vegetables, whole grains, and low-fat dairy products—typically provide more satiety with fewer calories because of their high water content. Energy-dense foods, on the other hand, are typically dry and are positively associated with total energy intakes of individuals and with the percent of energy in diets derived from sweeteners and fat. Dry foods with a stable shelf life are generally less costly, per calorie, than fresh, hydrated foods that spoil readily. Also, retail price increases over time for sweets and high-fat items are typically lower than for vegetables, fruit, and low-fat meats. In other words, the inverse relation between energy density and energy cost suggests that "obesity-promoting" foods are simply those that offer the most dietary energy at the lowest cost.

Food insecurity (limited or uncertain availability of nutritionally acceptable or safe foods), low income, and minority status are associated with obesity around the world. In the United States, women with low incomes and minority populations (except for Asian Americans) have higher rates of obesity than white males. A similar pattern is seen in economically depressed areas in Europe. Socioeconomic status may also have a greater impact on obesity in children than adults because preferences for energy-dense foods may be formed at an early age and are usually reinforced with repeated exposure to those foods and observation of parental eating habits. If sweet and high-fat foods are integral to a child's diet, as they tend to be in low-income families, preferences for those foods are likely to carry into adulthood and those adults may influence the habits of their own children.

Less Physical Activity

The amount of time children spend watching TV is positively correlated with obesity. Furthermore, physical activity, which typically declines with increased TV watching time, is inversely associated with childhood weight gain. Rates of physical activity worldwide are declining while TV viewing time is on the rise. In Great Britain, up to 69% of children spend less than 1 hour per day being moderately active. TV viewing time in that country is inversely correlated with levels of physical activity. A 2000 report from New Zealand found that TV viewing was positively associated with higher BMI, lower cardiovascular fitness, increased cigarette smoking, and elevated serum cholesterol in children and adults younger than the age of 26. In fact, in most countries where such data are available, physical activity levels are lower and TV viewing times are higher in youths who are overweight vs. normal weight.

Other Considerations

The prevalence of obesity in a country and community may also be linked to the variety and amounts of fruits and vegetables available to consumers, population density in urban areas, and transportation infrastructure. Availability of fresh fruits and vegetables was inversely correlated with obesity, especially in adult males, in a large study recently conducted on obesity patterns in Europe. Urban sprawl was positively associated with weight gain, as were poor public transportation systems. Presumably, in communities with urban sprawl, individuals are forced to drive to places of work and play instead of walking or riding a bike. Similarly, where public transportation is inadequate, people are more likely to drive to their destinations and miss out on walking to and from bus and train stations. This same study also found an inverse relationship with rates of obesity and the perceived effectiveness of government in producing sound social policies. Equally interesting was the positive relationship found between weight gain and perceived levels of government corruption. This, combined with all the other factors mentioned above, certainly makes a convincing argument for the complexity of the obesity epidemic.

Tackling the Problem

The trend for weight gain in human populations around the world seems to be due to the convergence of a perfect storm of factors. Physiologically, we are designed to crave sweets and fats; behaviorally, we tend to eat more if larger amounts and varieties of foods are presented to us; and we are literally shaped by our physical and cultural environments. Our economic status determines the types of foods available to us, and governmental policies certainly affect our lifestyles. We can't do much to change our essential nature. As a species, we will likely always crave high-calorie foods and overeat when the opportunity presents itself.

Factors in the greater environment, however, can be changed. Better community planning, with an emphasis on health promotion, could provide physical environments that encourage fitness. Improved public transportation systems, in addition to reducing traffic congestion and pollution, would necessitate more physical activity. Policy changes in schools and workplaces that eliminate the ubiquitous availability of energy-dense foods and snacks could significantly impact the number of calories children and adults consume.

The creation of programs in schools that encourage physical activity for a lifetime (less emphasis on organized and team sports, more emphasis on individual fitness) could encourage children and adolescents to move more throughout their life. Government recognition of the far-reaching impacts of poverty and its effect on public health may help create nutrition and other assistance programs that aid individuals in the purchase of healthier foods. Increased public and governmental awareness of the widening gap between wealthy and low-income individuals could help create economies and policies that alleviate hardship.

The excess calories produced by the large corporations and immense subsidies that characterize our current agricultural system will likely continue, as will the increasing availability of energy-dense foods in the global marketplace. Public nutrition education is needed to effect behavioral change and help individuals make informed choices. Researchers are looking to the model created by tobacco cessation programs for keys to the successful promotion of population-based lifestyle changes. The stages of change model for counseling used in cessation programs is largely effective in that regard. However, funding for nutrition education programs certainly does not come close to that available for smoking cessation programs, and the societal changes that have helped support a large reduction in tobacco use do not currently exist for habits involving food.

Perhaps a worldwide shift in values, prompted by changes in government, school, and workplace policies, will be necessary to truly turn the tide and help create thinner, healthier people.

> *"The nanny state's infatuation with an obesity epidemic that does not exist is a searing indictment of this particular public health crusade."*

The Obesity Epidemic Is a Myth

Patrick Basham and John Luik

Patrick Basham directs the Democracy Institute, an independent think tank, and is a scholar at the Cato Institute, a libertarian, public policy organization. John Luik is a senior fellow at the Democracy Institute. In the following viewpoint, Basham and Luik cite a 2010 report by the Centers for Disease Control and Prevention (CDC) in the United States and the Health Survey for England to refute the notion that these countries are suffering an obesity epidemic. The reports state that between 1999 and 2008, there has been a leveling off of obesity trends in the two countries. Basham and Luik insist that this evidence undermines current claims of an epidemic and reveals that governments are simply too eager to involve themselves in people's lives and to try to dictate "appropriate" lifestyles.

Patrick Basham and John Luik, "The Myth of an Obesity Tsunami," *Spiked*, January 2010. Reprinted by permission.

As you read, consider the following questions:

1. Over all the five time periods between 1999 and 2008 studied in the CDC report, which population group showed the only significant spike in weight gain, according to Basham and Luik?

2. As the authors report, by what percent has the number of overweight boys (aged two to ten) declined in England between 2005 and 2006?

3. What common culprit for childhood weight gain do Basham and Luik insist is blameless given the results of the CDC report and the English National Health survey?

Two studies produced by the US Centers for Disease Control and Prevention (CDC) and published last week [January 2010] in the *Journal of the American Medical Association*—one about obesity in children and adolescents, and the other about adult obesity—completely undermine the claims of an obesity epidemic.

Both studies are based on information from the National Health and Nutrition Examination Survey from 2007–08, which is a representative sample of the American population. The survey measured the heights and weights of 3,281 children and adolescents and 219 infants and toddlers, as well as 5,555 adult women and men. The study of children and adolescents looked at the body mass index (BMI) of children and adolescents over five time periods between 1999 and 2008, the decade during which child obesity was widely described as America's preeminent public health problem.

The results are striking. During none of the five periods was there a statistically significant trend, except for boys at the highest BMI levels. In other words, if there was a spike in obesity, it was confined to a very small number of very obese boys.

Obesity Declining or Leveling Off

What about the adult 'couch potato' generation? Here, again, the results put the lie to claims of an obesity tsunami. In the study of adults, the researchers also looked at obesity trends over the past decade. For women, there were no statistically significant changes in obesity prevalence over the entire decade, while for men there were no prevalence differences during the last five years of the decade. As the researchers note, obesity prevalence may have 'entered another period of relative stability'.

A similar absence of an obesity epidemic is to be found in England. According to the Health Survey for England, which collected data from 7,500 children and almost 7,000 adults, there has been a decline in the prevalence of overweight and obesity for adult men, while for adult women prevalence has remained the same.

Comparing the results of the survey for 2007 with those of 2004, there have been either declines or no significant changes in male prevalence of overweight and obesity in all age groups from 16–54. As for children, the survey finds: 'There was no significant change in mean BMI overweight/obesity prevalence between 2006 and 2007, and there are indications that the trend in obesity prevalence may have begun to flatten out over the last two to three years.'

For example, there was a decrease in obesity in girls aged two to 15 years old between 2005 and 2006, from 18 per cent in 2005 to 15 per cent in 2006. Among boys aged two to 10 years old, the prevalence of overweight declined from 16 per cent in 2005 to 12 per cent in 2006. According to the results, overweight and obesity have been declining amongst boys and girls aged two to 15 since 2004. In girls, obesity prevalence levels are largely unchanged from where they were in 2001.

Physical Activity Key

The findings of the English survey not only contradict the claim that we are in the midst of an obesity epidemic, but

77

they also debunk the public health establishment's erroneous claim that increases in children's weight are due to junkfood advertising and too many sugary soda drinks. According to the survey, the root cause of any weight gains that one does see appear to lie in physical activity levels. For example, '21 per cent of girls aged two to 15 in the low physical-activity group were classed as obese compared with 15 per cent of the high group'.

A similar pattern was found in the 2006 survey, which found that 33 per cent of girls aged two to 15 with low levels of physical activity were either overweight or obese compared with 27 per cent of those with high levels of physical activity. As with smoking, obesity prevalence was higher in both boys and girls in the lowest income group.

Clearly, governments' current course of draconian regulatory treatment seeks to cure an illusory disease. The nanny state's infatuation with an obesity epidemic that does not exist is a searing indictment of this particular public health crusade.

> "The NDM-1 gene has gone from being hardly detectable, to present in 1–3 per cent of all Indian patients with common gut bacterial infections—a 'staggering' increase."

The Indian Superbug NDM-1 Is a Growing Health Threat

Michael Hanlon

Michael Hanlon is a reporter for the Daily Mail, a UK newspaper. In the following viewpoint, Hanlon fears that the discovery and spread of a new bacterial gene in India could pose a significant health risk to the world. As Hanlon explains, the NDM 1 gene mutates common intestinal bacteria and provides them with resistance to modern antibiotics. Hanlon believes that the overprescription of antibiotics is responsible for the evolution of the drug-resistant "superbug," and he maintains that if the medical community does not change its prescription habits, more such diseases will arise to plague humanity. For now, though, Hanlon worries that the ease of transcontinental travel may spread the disease worldwide in a very short time.

Michael Hanlon, "We've Only Got Ourselves to Blame for the Indestructible Indian Superbug," *Daily Mail* (UK), August 2010. Reprinted by permission.

As you read, consider the following questions:

1. What are carbapenems, as Hanlon describes them?

2. What evidence does Hanlon give to support his claim that antibiotics have been overprescribed in recent decades?

3. According to the author, about how long could it take for science to develop new antibiotics to thwart the spread of the new superbug?

To discover just how grim the olden Days were, take a trip back to the 19th century. Witnessing the chronic misery and disease that touched everyone's lives back then, you will quickly realise just how important medicine's two greatest contributions to human welfare have been, namely mass vaccination and antibiotics—and give hearty thanks for the fact you live in the 21st century.

But now humanity faces the nightmarish prospect of losing one of them—and it's partly thanks to our own recklessness and profligacy [wastefulness].

This week [in August 2010], it is reported that a new strain of drug-resistant bacteria has emerged on the Indian subcontinent.

The germs in question are common gut bacteria, which have been modified by a gene called NDM-1 (New Delhi Metallobeta-lactamase-1).

Alarmingly, this modification makes bacteria such as E. coli completely resistant to all known antibiotics—even to the 'weapon of last resort', a group of drugs called the carbapenems, which are usually held in reserve for grave emergencies and infections by highly-resistant bacteria such as MRSA [methicillin-resistant *Staphylococcus aureus*].

More worryingly, the NDM-1 gene was found to be present on plasmids—bits of DNA which can easily be copied and transferred between different species of bacteria.

This suggests, according to the authors of the paper which was published in the *Lancet*, 'an alarming potential to spread and diversify among bacterial populations.'

Battling Evolving Microbes

For the best part of a century, doctors and the microbes have been engaged in an escalating, expensive and increasingly high-tech arms race.

Up to now, the medics have mostly had the upper hand, pulling, like rabbits out of a hat, clever new drugs, usually derived from various fungi and moulds (like Penicillin itself) which are a match for the latest strain of bacteria.

But there is a problem. No antibiotic, however potent, is ever completely effective. Like the (unintentionally) worrying TV ad for a disinfectant which 'kills 99 per cent of germs', it is the hard-as-nails 1 per cent that survive the chemical Armageddon that you have to worry about.

Bacteria reproduce, by dividing, at an alarming, exponential rate. And amid this promiscuity the bacteria's genes get spliced and transferred, and mutations are acquired and passed on.

While it can take centuries or millennia for an animal species to visibly evolve new traits, with bacteria new drug-resistant strains can emerge in months or even days, and spread like wildfire.

Ten years ago, it was the MRSA superbug that hit the headlines. The fear now is that something even nastier is emerging, a new group of drug resistant bacteria which really will spell the beginning of the end of the antibiotic era.

'People were predicting this five, ten years ago,' says Professor Mark Enright, an expert in superbugs, who works for a private biotech company developing novel ways to kill bacteria. 'The cat is now out of the bag.'

WHO Responds to NDM-1

The WHO [World Health Organization] recommended that governments step up surveillance for antimicrobial resistance and education on the appropriate use of antibiotics, stop the selling of antibiotics without a prescription, and promote strict adherence to infection control measures. The agency said these steps have proved effective in controlling resistant pathogens in many countries.

Robert Roos, CIDRAP, August 20, 2010. www.cidrap.umn.edu.

Reckless Human Actions

The evolution of the 'New Delhi' strain is unsurprising. Mass international travel and in particular medical tourism—which has seen thousands of people from wealthy countries travelling to places such as India and Pakistan, often for cheap plastic surgery—has led to the rapid evolution and spread of diseases such as this.

In just three years, the NDM-1 gene has gone from being hardly detectable, to present in 1–3 per cent of all Indian patients with common gut bacterial infections—a 'staggering' increase according to Professor Tim Walsh of Cardiff University, the lead author of the *Lancet*'s Infectious Diseases paper.

But we can't just blame the pernicious spread of medical tourism, often driven by vanity rather than need, for the emergence of this new strain. With antibiotics, humanity as a whole has been utterly reckless.

Knowing what we know now, if we could go back in time we would have prescribed antibiotics sparingly and only when they were really needed.

If we had done that, we may not have been facing the prospect of superbugs for the next 100 years.

Antibiotics Prescribed Too Often

Instead, antibiotics have been massively overprescribed, thrown willy-nilly at patients by harassed and time-pressed doctors for a host of minor ailments—often coughs and colds that aren't even caused by bacteria in the first place.

As Professor Enright says: 'Every time you throw enough antibiotics at enough people, you encourage the evolution of drug-resistant mutants.'

This happens everywhere, from GP [general practice] surgeries in Britain and the U.S.—where antibiotics are the medicine of choice for just about every minor childhood snuffle—to India, where antibiotics are available cheaply over the counter without a prescription.

Here, there is no need for even a rudimentary diagnosis. They are guzzled by millions every day.

So, what can be done? In India, as Professor Enright says, probably nothing; the cat is, indeed, out of the bag.

In the UK, only comprehensive monitoring and, if necessary, isolation and quarantine are likely to be effective.

Sadly, these measures are not cheap and in an increasingly cash-strapped NHS [National Health Services] unlikely to be adopted with any rigour.

Some doctors have called for all patients who have received medical treatment in India to be screened on arrival in their home country. Several cases of NDM-1 have been found in British patients who went to India for both urgent medically needed surgery and cosmetic procedures.

Such a measure would undoubtedly be sensible. But, unfortunately, screening those returning globetrotters who hold UK passports would present probably insurmountable legal and financial hurdles.

Future Safeguards Are Needed

Fortunately, the bacteria in question (unlike the staphylococcus MRSA strain) are not particularly virulent. We are not going to see a wave of deaths among otherwise healthy people as a result of drug-resistant E.coli, for instance.

But for people in hospital, with weakened immune systems and with infected wounds, this could turn into a real issue.

Ultimately, we will need new antibiotics—and even completely new ways of killing bacteria.

Professor Enright's team at Biocontrol Ltd are working on a new take on an old idea—using natural viruses to attack bacteria instead of antibiotics.

Clinical trials are under way and we could have a new weapon in our armoury within three to ten years.

Sadly, developing new antibiotics is both expensive and financially unrewarding.

While a new painkiller or anti-inflammatory drug can make a drug company billions, a new antibiotic, especially one which by its very nature should be held in reserve and only prescribed in small quantities, will probably not turn a profit for anyone.

As with vaccines (which are also expensive to develop, and often generate little return) we need a new economic model for the development of such drugs.

We also need to rethink the policy of sending patients abroad for operations.

It is easy to imagine that in a few decades we will look back upon the era from 1940 to maybe the 2020s as a golden age, one in which we had infectious disease at bay.

Maybe we will find yet another rabbit to pull out of the hat; human ingenuity knows, after all, few bounds. But if not, we probably have only our own profligacy to blame.

In the war against the bacteria, humanity would have done well to keep its powder dry.

Periodical and Internet Sources Bibliography

The following articles have been selected to supplement the diverse views presented in this chapter.

George Alleyne	"HIV/AIDS: Will We Win And When?" *UN Chronicle*, 2010.
Regina M. Benjamin	"Obesity Epidemic: What Needs to Be Done—Now," *Ebony*, June 2010.
Corrie Brown	"Fighting the Rise of Emerging Infectious Diseases," *USA Today* magazine, May 2010.
W. Wayt Gibbs	"Obesity: An Overblown Epidemic?" *Scientific American*, June 2005.
Christian Gladel	"The World's Best Hope to End the AIDS Epidemic," *UN Chronicle*, June–August 2006.
Danylo Hawaleshka, Cathy Gulli, and Nicholas Köhler	"The Allergy Epidemic," *Maclean's*, June 5, 2006.
Debora MacKenzie	"The End of Civilisation," *New Scientist*, April 5, 2008.
Sara Reistad-Long	"Our Biggest Health Threat," *Woman's Day*, October 2010.
Shirley S. Wang and Katherine Hobson	"Gene Makes 'Superbugs' Resistant to Drugs," *Wall Street Journal*, August 12, 2010.
Mortimer B. Zuckerman	"A Nightmare Scenario," *U.S. News & World Report*, June 27, 2005.

CHAPTER 2

How Serious Was the Threat of an H1N1 Swine Flu Pandemic?

Chapter Preface

In April 2009, Mexican officials reported an outbreak of H1N1 influenza (swine flu) in the country's capital. Within a month eight hundred people in Mexico had been diagnosed with the disease, and forty-two died from it. More than a thousand cases began popping up in countries throughout the world, compelling the World Health Organization (WHO) to raise its preparedness standing to phase 5, a degree of alert that had not been witnessed since the warning system had been implemented in response to avian flu in 2005. In an April 29, 2009, *New York Times* article, Dr. Margaret Chan, director-general of the WHO, was quoted as advising, "All countries should immediately activate their pandemic preparedness plans." Indeed, within two months, Chan issued a follow-up statement that the WHO had raised the warning level to phase 6, indicating that swine flu had become pandemic after more than thirty thousand cases of the contagion had been reported in seventy-four countries. In that same statement, Chan assured, "WHO has been in close dialogue with influenza vaccine manufacturers. I understand that production of vaccines for seasonal influenza will be completed soon, and that full capacity will be available to ensure the largest possible supply of pandemic vaccine in the months to come."

By August 2009, however, vaccine shortfalls were apparent. The United States expected 120 million doses to have been prepared in the months after the June warning, but officials had to revise the count to around 45 million. Global production of the vaccine was estimated to reach 4.9 billion doses for the year, but manufacturing problems reduced the number to around 94 million. The dearth caused anxiety among the billions of people who anticipated that the WHO's dire prophecy would come true and the pandemic would spread across the globe. Instead, the disease remained confined mostly in well-off nations where health officials rapidly quarantined those infected. Swine flu failed to penetrate developing countries where the lack of health care could easily have caused greater devastation.

By February 2010, health officials were predicting that the threat of swine flu had reached its peak and would begin tapering off. Richard Knox, the science and health correspondent for National Public Radio, told listeners in a February 18 broadcast that the disease was not as virulent as expected in the United States. "About 57 million Americans got this new H1N1 flu between last April and January," Knox said. "And that's really probably about as many as get the flu in a severe flu season—a regular one, not a pandemic season." Some critics began accusing the WHO of overreacting to the threat of the swine flu, and others claimed the WHO inflated the danger to benefit the drug companies that supposedly were paying kickbacks to WHO researchers. Despite the controversy, the WHO ultimately declared the swine flu pandemic over on August 10, 2010. Globally, the disease killed more than eighteen thousand people, a figure much smaller than the death toll from other seasonal flu viruses.

The debate over the potential threat of swine flu and the reaction of health authorities to the pandemic is played out in the following chapter. Here, experts and pundits discuss the WHO's rush to classify the disease as a pandemic as well as the assertions that health organizations and vaccine manufacturers inflate public fears to bilk nervous governments of millions of dollars.

| "Americans believe that the flu threat was overblown and the pandemic is over. . ."

H1N1 Was Never a Serious Threat to World Health

Daniel J. Ncayiyana

Daniel J. Ncayiyana is editor of the South African Medical Journal. *In the following viewpoint, Ncayiyana claims that Americans believe the swine flu pandemic was overblown by the World Health Organization (WHO). He explains that there are those who believe the WHO overstated the threat of H1N1 and raised a false alarm. The big pharmacuetical companies stood to make huge profits from such a claim and some speculate that the WHO changed the terms under which a pandemic may be declared.*

As you read, consider the following questions:

1. As of June 2009, how many people worldwide had the H1N1 flu strain infected?

2. How much money did France spend on obtaining enough of the H1N1 vaccine for its entire population?

Daniel J. Ncayiyana, "H1N1 Hype a Treasure Trove for Conspiracy Theorists," *South African Medical Journal*, March 2010. Reproduced by permission.

3. As stated in the article, what does World Health Organization Dr. Keiji Fukuda maintain about the WHO's definition of influenza pandemics?

In June 2009, the World Health Organization (WHO) declared the influenza H1N1 virus a pandemic, the first such pandemic to be declared in 41 years. At that time, the new strain had infected 28 000 people worldwide, with 141 fatalities. Since then the pandemic has turned out to be a bit of a damp squib for much of the global public. Americans believe that the flu threat was overblown and the pandemic is over, and therefore do not intend to get the swine flu vaccine being pushed by US public health authorities, according to a recent poll of the Harvard School of Public Health. To date, only one-fifth of the US population has been vaccinated. Vaccine uptake has been similarly unenthusiastic elsewhere in the world.

Americans could perhaps be excused for being sceptical about the vaccine. Back in the 1970s, with the anticipation of an imminent outbreak of an earlier variant of H1N1, US President Gerald Ford's administration rolled out a massive campaign to vaccinate every man, woman and child in the US against what was then also known as swine flu. The epidemic failed to materialise, but the vaccine was linked to an outbreak of Guillain-Barre syndrome that cost many lives, causing the campaign to be abandoned.

Overstating the H1N1 Pandemic

Did the WHO overstate the threat of an H1N1 pandemic? There are those who think so. Dr Wolfgang Wodarg, a member of the German parliament and chair of the Parliamentary Assembly of the Council of Europe's health committee, bluntly contends that 'WHO advised us falsely; they raised a false alarm.' Then there are those who believe that the timing of the WHO's declaration of a pandemic was contrived to benefit the big pharmaceutical companies that stood to make huge gains from such a declaration.

That big pharma did in fact benefit substantially from the declaration of a pandemic is beyond question. In response to the earlier emergence of SARS and the H5N1 avian flu and the panic they caused, most Western countries had taken steps to set up contingency plans to prepare for possible future outbreaks of other deadly pandemics. The plans included signing up to multi-billion dollar advance-purchase agreements with pharmaceutical companies for the supply of vaccines, that would automatically kick in if a deadly pandemic was declared by the WHO. These plans all envisaged a worst-case scenario. The UK's plan, for example, predicted between 50 000 and 750 000 deaths from such a flu pandemic. So far, however, there have been 400 British deaths from H1N1. In any event, when the WHO declared the H1N1 pandemic, these contracts were immediately activated and, as one conspiracy bloggist puts it, 'Once a "pandemic" is declared it is basically a license for pharma to print money. Great business model!' France alone spent $1.5 billion on procuring enough of the vaccine to inoculate its entire population of 60 million. However, with little demand for vaccination from the public, France and many other Western countries are now stuck with massive H1N1 vaccine surpluses and are scrambling to find ways to unload them.

Change in Terms?

But how did this come about? Did the WHO fiddle with its own definitions in declaring an H1N1 pandemic? There is some evidence that the WHO did in fact subtly change the terms under which such a pandemic may be declared. 'Before the arrival of novel A/H1N1 virus,' writes Doshi in the BMJ, 'pandemics were said to occur when a new subtype of influenza virus to which humans have no immunity enters the population, begins spreading widely, and causes severe illness.

A Media Fear Campaign

Across the mainstream media, reports announce one swine flu death after another....

The media has never been in the habit of reporting the cases of people who, for no known reason, die of the flu. Out of the 35,000 Americans who die each year from flu-related illnesses, some are bound to be relatively young and healthy. It happens. This year, however, their stories are front-page news.

Source: Andrew Bosworth,
"Exposed: The Swine Flue Hoax,"
LewRockwell.com, August 26, 2009.
www.lewrockwell.com.

WHO, for example, for years defined pandemics as outbreaks causing "enormous numbers of deaths and illness", but in early May, removed this phrase from the definition.' WHO's Dr Keiji Fukuda, however, maintains that WHO's definition of influenza pandemics has always been based on transmissibility and has never had anything to do with the lethality of a virus. No matter; conspiracy theorists predictably pounced on the definitional change as the 'smoking gun' that proves WHO's complicity in the alleged machinations by the pharmaceutical industry.

The charge of a conspiracy does not ring true. And as *Time* magazine puts it, 'it is not difficult to imagine an alternate scenario in which critics would now be accusing the agency of failing to warn countries properly of the H1N1 threat' if the worst had come to the worst. This may still come about; H1N1 has not been wiped off the face of the earth yet. More lethal waves of the flu may still lie ahead.

"*Just because swine flu turned out to be a non-event, that doesn't mean that we should conclude that our technology is at fault and that it is a mistake to try to anticipate future disasters.*"

H1N1 Could Have Posed a Serious Threat to World Health

Mark Honigsbaum

In the following viewpoint, Mark Honigsbaum, a researcher at the Wellcome Trust Centre for the History of Medicine at University College London and the author of Living with Enza: The Forgotten Story of Britain and the Great Flu Pandemic of 1918, *argues that preparations for a swine flu pandemic were appropriate despite the fact that the disease was not as virulent as predicted. Honigsbaum asserts that preparing for worst-case scenarios is how health organizations and governments protect their citizens, and in this case, such preparations might have been needed had H1N1 posed a serious threat. He believes that the rampant accusations that governments overreacted or conspired to hype the disease are unfounded and smack of anti-science thinking.*

Mark Honigsbaum, "Swine Flu Could Have Been a Disaster," *Guardian* (UK), January 30, 2010. Reprinted by permission.

As you read, consider the following questions:

1. How many doses of Tamiflu did the English government order, according to Honigsbaum?

2. As the author reports, what did Louis Farrakhan argue was the "real purpose" of the H1N1 vaccine?

3. According to Honigsbaum, why do some health-advice websites tell mothers to avoid giving the swine flu vaccine to their children?

Swine flu is no longer sickening very many people but that does not mean it is no longer newsworthy. On the contrary, in recent weeks [at the end of 2009 and beginning of 2010] a succession of critics have rounded on "happy-go-lucky" virologists, "headline-hungry" journalists and the World Health Organisation [WHO], accusing them of being variously dupes of the pharmaceutical industry or willing accomplices to pointless hysteria. Their crime? Hyping the pandemic that never was and thereby helping Big Pharma to a billion-dollar vaccine bonanza.

Leading the told-you-so's is Dr Wolfgang Wodarg, the former head of the Council of Europe's health committee, who this week [in late January 2010] tabled a motion in Strasbourg [France] accusing the WHO of having "faked" the pandemic. Another is the [British newspaper the] *Guardian's* Simon Jenkins. In characteristically acerbic prose he rails against government scientists for peddling "drivel" about the tens of thousands of Britons who might have died this winter. That they didn't and that you and I are still alive shows that H1N1 is not the "Andromeda strain" long-predicted by scientists. "It was pure, systematic, government-induced panic," he writes. "Swine flu was a textbook case of a scare," concurs Christopher Booker in [Britain's] *Daily Telegraph*.

Lingering Swine Flu Worries

Even with infection rates dropping, many flu experts are concerned about some facets of swine flu. While mortality is low, children make up many of the victims. And even though [the 2011] seasonal flu vaccine will likely include protection against swine flu, virulent new strains could emerge.

Arlene Weintraub et al., Bloomberg BusinessWeek, *February 4, 2010. www.businessweek.com.*

An Inexact Science

Jenkins is a sharp and entertaining writer and when he accuses the media of playing "its joyful part" in propagating panic I have to admit the dart hits home: as a medical historian and expert on the 1918 "Spanish" influenza pandemic I was continually asked to comment on the parallels with swine flu last summer [2009] and no doubt added to the hype. But as all good schoolboys know, *post hoc* doesn't make *propter hoc* [Latin for "after this thing, because of this thing"; meaning "just because a prior event occurred, it does not follow that a subsequent event was caused by the prior event"]. Just because 65,000 Britons didn't die this winter does not mean that the computer models were wrong or that the Department of Health shouldn't have ordered 50m[illion] doses of Tamiflu, only that prognostications about pandemics, like prognostications about earthquakes, are not an exact science.

Writing in this paper [the *Guardian*] last week, Tom Sheldon eloquently makes the point that predicting pandemics is a species of risk analysis and thus, by definition, subject to error. With better virological and epidemiological data perhaps the government wouldn't have stockpiled so much Tamiflu or ordered 90m doses of vaccine. But if it hadn't and armageddon had occurred, Jenkins would have been the first to call for the guillotining of the Chief Medical Officer.

Unwarranted Conspiracy Theories

I do not wish to labour the point but it seems to me that the backlash against swine flu is a species of conspiracy-thinking, one that wilfully misconstrues the role of science in the regulation of technologies of health which have brought so many benefits to society. In the same way that 9/11 denialists point to the collapse of World Trade Centre 7 to support their wacko theories about "controlled demolitions", swine flu denialists point to [former US Secretary of Defense] Donald Rumsfeld's position on the board of Gilead, the company that developed Tamiflu, to argue that the "panic" was got up by similar shadowy neo-conservative corporate interests. It is then a short step to seeing all such panics as conspiracies. Thus, according to the Nation of Islam leader Louis Farrakhan, the vaccine is really a tool for culling inner-city black populations because of military leaders' concerns about pressures on the global food supply.

Similar conspiracy-thinking infects health advice websites that advise mothers not to give their children the swine flu jab because of the risk of rare side-effects, such as Guillain-Barré syndrome [GBS; an autoimmune disorder]. In fact, according to the Institute of Medicine, the chances of contracting GBS from influenza vaccination is one or two per million. By comparison, a recent French study found that the risk of contracting GBS from naturally occurring influenza is four to seven out of every 100,000 cases. But that hasn't stopped [England's] NHS [National Health Services] staff, who should know better, from shunning the swine flu vaccine. Nor, I am sorry to say, are such peer-reviewed studies likely to persuade the sort of people who continue to refuse to give their children the

MMR [measles, mumps, and rubella] vaccine because they once read somewhere that it might be linked to autism.

Better Safe than Sorry

Twenty years ago, writing in the context of a very different epidemic, one that to date has claimed two million lives worldwide, Susan Sontag warned that the modern ability to anticipate and estimate the scale of future disasters had resulted in two very different visions of apocalypse: "There is what is happening now. And there is what it portends: the imminent, but not yet actual, and not really graspable, disaster." The result was what Sontag called a "permanent modern scenario: apocalypse looms . . . and it doesn't occur."

Sontag, of course, was writing in the context of Aids and Jenkins is quite right to point out that in the response to swine flu there has been a similar inflation of apocalyptic rhetoric. But just because swine flu turned out to be a non-event, that doesn't mean that we should conclude that our technology is at fault and that it is a mistake to try to anticipate future disasters. As Margaret Chan, the director of the World Health Organisation, acknowledged in June [2009] when she issued a "phase six" alert, triggering the drawdown on the government's stockpile of Tamiflu, "the virus writes the rules and this one, like all influenza viruses, can change the rules, without rhyme or reason, at any time".

> *"The swine flu frenzy . . . was commenced and amplified by the U.S. government and its hordes of international lackeys."*

The Government Manufactured the H1N1 Threat

Karen DeCoster

Karen DeCoster is an accounting and financial professional and a special advisor to the Clare Boothe Luce Policy Institute, an organization of politically conservative women. In the viewpoint that follows, DeCoster claims that the H1N1 swine flu epidemic was a hoax perpetrated by the government. DeCoster asserts that the government manufactured hysteria over the disease to enrich pharmaceutical companies, which, in turn, paid kickbacks to politicians. She maintains that the government tried to impose vaccinations and even sanitary regulations upon the public in order to build fear and cow people into accepting that the cost of the millions of vaccines and hand sanitizers was a necessary expense to fight an alleged threat. DeCoster insists that the public eventually caught on to the lie when far fewer people died of swine flu than the government predicted.

Karen DeCoster, "Revisiting the Swine Flu Lies and Hysteria," The John Birch Society, January 2010. Reprinted by permission.

As you read, consider the following questions:

1. As DeCoster asserts, what was the August 2009 CDC estimate of the number of fatalities that might result from swine flu?

2. According to the author, what did the Department of Homeland Security supposedly consider rationing if the swine flu began sickening huge numbers of Americans?

3. How much taxpayer money did the US government spend on swine flu vaccinations, according to DeCoster?

Along with the U.S. government's numerous military entanglements, there are a series of "smaller" wars that the state carries out against the people who reside within its borders. These "wars" all bear the crisis logo, and they are always targeted at protecting you from something—real, exaggerated, or contrived—that requires massive government intervention and the curtailment of liberties in order to win the war.

The Government's Latest War

The war on the swine flu has been an ongoing affair for the government-media partnership that turned this issue into the most overrated story of 2009. Government officials, up to and including the president, have placed a disproportionate amount of emphasis on a barely notable strain of flu and have used it as justification for embarking on a health jihad that has come to dominate American society. Thanks to this latest offensive, America is chock-full of hallway hand sanitizers in corporate and public buildings; mini-hand sanitizers being passed around like a tin of mints; and posters stuck everywhere telling you how to sneeze, cough, breathe, and properly wash your hands. The Henson Company even produced a collectivist and creepy propaganda piece for children [on the television show *Sid the Science Kid*], urging them to get a flu shot for the good of the community.

It is true that a gaggle of faithful followers lined up to offer their bodies—and the bodies of their children—as guinea pigs for the H1N1 vaccine that had never been fully tested. They lined up at sites where the vaccine first became available. As time went on, however, public opinion was swayed by an abundance of evidence that the issue was being oversold in order to build a watershed of crisis and fear. Americans began to refuse the vaccinations, and in fact, many people started speaking out against them as they questioned the vaccine's necessity and safety.

A National Hysteria Campaign

The swine flu frenzy that was commenced and amplified by the U.S. government and its hordes of international lackeys has been a splendid example of misusing propaganda to build hysteria to such an excessive degree that it not only becomes ineffective, but it becomes counterproductive. The mingling of tempered reality with unrestrained fantasy to a degree where the assertions become almost comical leads those who are being propagandized to view the embellishments as serving a divergent and possibly sinister cause.

For instance, in August of 2009, the CDC [Centers for Disease Control and Prevention] released a report that stated the swine flu pandemic could cause up to 90,000 deaths. This report would help to serve a justification for the government's massive fear mongering campaign, including early indications that there would be mandatory vaccinations. In late October, the CDC reported about 1,000 deaths from the swine flu, and two weeks later the CDC reported 4,000 deaths. How is that possible? Did 3,000 people die between late October and early November? The CDC spun the story this way: earlier numbers being used were giving the government "an incomplete story of the pandemic." The CDC's original count included only laboratory confirmed cases, while its new numbers included estimates from epidemiologists. This way, the numbers could be gamed and a story of far greater severity could be peddled to the public. This all came about at a time when the swine flu numbers were already taking a nosedive and not living up to the government's bullish pandemic predictions.

Perhaps the most comical scaremongering ruse in the whole swine flu circus was the Department of Homeland Security's contingency plans to ration Internet bandwidth and block websites to avoid a possible overrun of Internet provider capacity should too many Americans come down with the swine flu and stay home to surf the Internet all day.

As the flu tizzy has wound down and started to disappear from the media headlines, I have been waiting patiently for a perspective to appear in mainstream print that refuses to let go of the hysteria, and instead attempts to amplify it. The *Wall Street "Swine Flu" Journal* doesn't disappoint:

> Global health officials' response to the swine-flu pandemic reflects major improvements in flu-fighting capabilities in recent years, but limited vaccine supplies, crowded emergency rooms, and other challenges show they still aren't fully equipped to combat a deadlier scourge, the World Health Organization's [WHO] chief said.

> While a second wave of infections caused by the H1N1 virus has ebbed in North America and Western Europe, transmission of flu remains intense in Central and Eastern Europe and parts of southern Asia, and health authorities must monitor its spread for another year or more, WHO Director-General Margaret Chan said in an interview this week.

> "It is premature to say the pandemic has peaked worldwide," she said. "The situation needs to be watched and monitored at least another six to 12 months." The virus could still mutate to become more severe, she warned.

State bureaucrats 'round the world, and especially in the U.S., can't stand it. They are absolutely disappointed that their perfidious pandemic was a bust, a flop, and a non-pandemic.

The Hoax Is Apparent

If people would simply shut off the CDC's supported propaganda noise being blasted across the airwaves and newspapers . . . and simply do their homework, Americans would wake up and realize the hoax behind the swine flu pandemic. All of the information is before us. Nothing is hidden. All the contradictions and hypocrisies are contained within the massive vaccine industrial complex—including the government health agencies and professional medical associations. The lie is too large for them to not expose themselves if we simply look.

Richard Gale and Gary Null, Health Freedom USA,
October 26, 2009. www.heatlhfreedomusa.org.

Of course, there are no limited vaccine supplies or over-whelmed emergency rooms—that was a liar's cacophony for the purpose of using the swine flu epidemic as a control mechanism.

Pushing a Vaccine No One Wants

Currently, what I am seeing from the press is a bunch of inept fear mongering about a "third wave" of the swine flu—and this comes at a point when the general public long ago lost interest in the so-called "second wave." The CBS Connecticut website ran a "third wave" bulletin that says since a third wave is "possible," people should still be vaccinated. Federal despots, unwilling to be left out of either wave and the ensuing disinformation fever, have chimed in with the CDC's warning of a third wave in January [2010]. The story states, "The CDC reports fewer people getting sick. That may not be the case come January." Remind me of what happened to the "second wave," or even the first?

I am amused each time I go into a Walgreens, or drive by a CVS, health clinic, doctor's office, or urgent care center. They all have signs in the windows, on the doors, and even outside in front of their buildings: "H1N1—get your shots here." No one wants the vaccination so they have to push it and advertise it. Next thing you know they'll be doing "buy one get one free" H1N1 shots or having blue light specials. In fact, many places are already giving away free vaccines. Isn't this the same vaccination for which the U.S. government declared—over and over and over—there would be an extreme shortage, and we must all hurry and get it if such an opportunity appears? Again and again, Americans were being conditioned to believe that there was an undisputed, full-scale, worldwide health emergency that would soon mushroom into an uncontrollable killer flu, and our chances of being victims of some hideous health horror were higher than tripping and stubbing your toe.

Government, along with its obedient media arm, perpetually warned Americans of massive deaths, overrun hospitals, a shortage of lung machines, and the lack of available medical personnel to handle the massive overrun of resources that would be the result of a ginormous swine flu outbreak. Every day, every hour, the *Swine Flu Journal*, the *Swine Flu Times*, the *Swine Flu Post* [respectively, the *Wall Street Journal, New York Times*, and *Washington Post*], and all of those other organs of fear mongering and swine journalism, kept us up to date with play-by-plays of the expected date of H1N1 vaccination arrivals, the current shortage, and the expected time frames to relieve the shortage. Zillions of dollars were put into the pockets of the large and powerful Big Pharma interests who lobbied to sell the swine flu as a killer affliction and paid off scores of politicians and health bureaucrats to have it declared a pandemic. The U.S. government spent at least $2 billion dollars on vaccinations for Americans so that every single American could suck up Big Pharma's moneymaking toxic juice.

A Hoax to Enrich Special Interests

A study recently concluded by researchers at Harvard University and the Medical Research Council Biostatistics Unit in the U.K. revealed that the spring 2009 flu cases signaled a flu season that might be only slightly worse than normal. Philip Alcabes, author of *Dread: How Fear and Fantasy Have Fueled Epidemics from the Black Death to Avian Flu*, while commenting on this study, stated in an interview on ABC News,

> "I think that it was, from the very beginning, created as a crisis and overstated as a real threat," he said, adding that he did not want to understate the seriousness of influenza.

> "Flu is a serious illness, it kills people," he said. But, he added, "It does a disservice to public health when, in the name of a preparedness crusade, people create a narrative of crisis or catastrophe before we have enough data that this is happening."

The swine flu panic was a profligate hoax on the part of government autocrats and special interests—spearheaded by Big Pharma and the medical establishment—that stood to profit from its existence. A strain of flu was defined as a death-dealing pandemic in order to develop a rationale for launching a sweeping campaign of health tyranny against American citizens while corporate state interests stood to benefit hugely from the terror campaign.

In spite of holding all the cards, the government's swine flu scheme failed miserably. It failed because enough people had the backbone to stop listening to the tripe that dominated the public airwaves. The fizzle and flop was similar to the one that occurred, recently, in a Nigerian's underwear somewhere over Detroit [i.e., the Nigerian bomber who smuggled explosives in his underwear onto a transatlantic jetliner on December 25, 2009, which failed to detonate]. The whole thing fell flat on its face because the totalitarian government of Washington D.C. overplayed the drama and fear, and, like a broken record, its orders, advice, and dictates began to sound more and more like vaudeville one-liners.

| "*Governments . . . do not create new diseases, spread them, or sustain them.*"

The Government Did Not Manufacture the H1N1 Threat

Sam Vaknin

Sam Vaknin is a columnist for Global Politician, PopMatters, and other websites. In the following viewpoint, Vaknin argues that the government did not conspire with big pharmaceutical companies to create the H1N1 swine flu scare. Though Vaknin agrees that epidemics are good for the pharmaceutical business, he points out that the companies must overcome their huge initial research and testing costs. Government collusion might aid the profits of drug companies, but since the pharmaceutical industry must rely on government contracts ironed out ahead of time, Vaknin insists it is difficult to assume that politicians can predict when the next disease threat will arise. Vaknin asserts that the desire to blame government and drug companies for profiteering has more to do with a general distrust of these institutions coupled with a unique public fascination with conspiracy theories.

Sam Vaknin, "Swine Flu as a Conspiracy," *Global Politician*, November 2009. Reprinted by permission.

As you read, consider the following questions:

1. Why does Vaknin insist that the $8 billion to $18 billion in vaccines and other antiflu drugs is "a drop in the industry's bucket" in terms of profits?

2. How much money did GlaxoSmithKline, the makers of the swine flu vaccine, amass from vaccine sales by the end of 2009, according to the author?

3. Who does Vaknin blame for the origin of new diseases and pandemics?

The Internet has rendered global gossip that in previous epochs would have remained local. It [has] also allowed rumour-mongers to leverage traditional and trusted means of communication—texts and images—to lend credence to the most outlandish claims. Some bloggers and posters have not flinched from doctoring photos and video clips. Still, the most efficient method of disseminating disinformation and tall tales in the wild is via text.

In May 2009, as swine flu was surging through the dilapidated shanties of Mexico, I received a mass-distribution letter from someone claiming to have worked at the National Institutes of Health [NIH] in Virology: "I worked in the Laboratory of Structural Biology Research under the NIAMS [National Institute of Arthritis, Musculoskeletal, and Skin Diseases] division of NIH from 2002–2004." Atypically, the source provided a name, an e-mail address, and a phone number. He stated that the newly-minted pandemic was the outcome of a "recombinant virus [that] has been unleashed upon mankind" by a surrealistic coalition: "the Executive Branch of our (USA) government, the World Health Organization (WHO), as well as Baxter Pharmaceutical," the latter being "involved in international biological weapons programs." The media was lying blatantly about the number of casualties.

"Media Panic Pandemic," by Jose Nemo-Neves. www.CartoonStock.com

The e-mail letter cautioned against "a martial law type scenario" in which the government will "ban public gatherings, enforce travel restrictions . . . forced vaccination or forced quarantine." He advised people to hoard food, obtain N95 or P100 masks, and "Have a means of self-defense." Tamiflu and, more generally, neuraminidase inhibitors are not effective, he warned. Instead, he recommended organic food (including garlic), drops of Colloidal Silver Hydrosol, Atomic (nascent) iodine, Allicin, Medical Grade, and NAC (N-acetyl-cysteine).

Suspicion of Government and Big Pharma

Blaming government and the pharmaceutical industry for instigating the very diseases they are trying to contain and counter is old hat. It is founded on the dubious assertion of cui bono [who will benefit?]: pandemics are worth anywhere from 8 to 18 billion USD in extra annual income from the enhanced sales of vaccines, anti-virals, antibiotics, wipes, masks, sanitizers, and the like. That's a drop in the industry's bucket (close to 1 trillion USD in sales last year [2008]), yet it comes in handy in times of economic slowdown. Luckily for the drug-makers, most major epidemics and pandemics have occurred during recessions, perfectly timed to shore their balance sheets.

The sales or profits of drug-makers not involved in the swine flu panic (such as Pfizer) actually went down in the third quarter of 2009 as opposed to the revenues and net income of those who were. Novartis expects to make an extra 400–700 million USD in the last quarter of 2009 and first quarter of 2010. Sanofi-Aventis has sold a mere 120 million worth of swine flu related goods, but this will shoot up to 1 billion in the six months to March 2010. Similarly, while Astra-Zeneca's tally is a meagre 152 million USD, yet it constitutes 2% of its growth and one third of its sales in the USA. It foresees another 300 million USD in revenues. Finally, Glaxo-SmithKline has pushed a whopping 1.6 billion USD worth of swine flu vaccine out the door plus an extra 250 million USD in related products till end-of-September 2009. Pandemics are good for business, no two ways about it.

The aura of the pharmaceutical industry is such that people seamlessly lump it together with weapons manufacturers, the CIA, Big Tobacco, and other usual culprits and suspects. Drug manufacturers' advertising budgets are huge and may exert disproportionate influence on editorial decisions in the print media. Pharma companies are big contributors to campaign coffers and can and do bend politicians' ears in times of need. There is a thinly-veiled revolving door between underpaid and over-worked bureaucrats in regulatory agencies and the plush offices of the ostensibly regulated. Academic studies are often funded by the industry. People naturally are suspicious and apprehensive of this confluence of power, money, and access. Recent scandals at the FDA (America's much-vaunted and hitherto-venerated Food and Drug Administration) did not help matters.

Government and Drug Companies Do Not Create Diseases

The truth is that pharmaceutical companies are very reluctant to develop vaccines, or to cope with pandemics, whose sufferers are often the indigent inhabitants of developing and poor countries. To amortize their huge sunk costs (mainly in research and development) they resort to supply-side and demand-side measures.

On the demand side, they often insist on advance market commitments: guaranteed purchases by governments, universities, and NGOs [nongovernmental organizations]. They also enjoy tax credits and breaks, grants, and awards. Differential pricing is used to skew decision-making and re-allocate the economic resources of the governments of impoverished countries in favour of purchasing larger quantities of products such as vaccines. On the supply side, they create artificial scarcity by patenting the processes that are involved in the production of vaccines and drugs; by licencing technologies only to a handful of carefully-placed factories; and by producing under the maximum capacity so as to induce rationing within tight release and delivery schedules (which, in itself, induces panic).

Still, collude as they may in profiteering, governments and the pharma industry do not create new diseases, spread them, or sustain them. This job is best left to the poor and the ignorant whose living conditions encourage cross-species infections and whose superstitions foment hysteria every time a new strain of virus is discovered. You can count on them to render the rich drug-manufacturer even richer every single time.

> *"Many of the scientists who . . . are presented as 'independent experts' . . . carefully conceal the fact that they receive money from pharmaceutical companies."*

Pharmaceutical Companies Paid Health Experts to Hype the H1N1 Threat

Rudi C. Loehwing

Rudi C. Loehwing is a member of the British House of Lords and the managing director of the World Institute of Natural Health Sciences, a nonprofit organization that advocates for the natural and alternative medical science field. In the following viewpoint, Loehwing accuses the drug industry of paying off health officials to hype the H1N1 swine flu pandemic. He contends that several accounts have been made public of officials within the World Health Organization taking pay from pharmaceutical companies manufacturing swine flu vaccines and preventative drugs. He also contends that the drug industry has powerful lobbyists in Washington, D.C., influencing the health policies of the United States. Loehwing believes this conflict of interest should compel authorities to remove anyone in the pay

Rudi C. Loehwing, "H1N1 Swine Flu Vaccines Driven by Illegal Graft and Pay Offs," *Your Story*, August 2010. Reprinted by permission.

of pharmaceutical companies from directing or mandating international or national health procedures.

As you read, consider the following questions:

1. How much money does Loehwing say Juhani Eskola received from GlaxoSmithKline to research vaccines in 2009?

2. Who is nicknamed "Dr. Flu," and why does the author indict him?

3. What "charity"-related plan does Loehwing revile as a means for big pharmaceutical companies to influence private-practice physicians?

In yet another exposé of the financial corruption that is driving the H1N1 "pandemic" and pharmaceutical vaccine scam, a Finnish member of the World Health Organization Board, who also happens to be one of their key advisors on pharmaceutical vaccines, has allegedly received 6 million Euros from the vaccine manufacturer GlaxoSmithKline. Although the World Health Organization (WHO) promised full transparency, this conflict of interest has only recently been uncovered through much effort.

Professor Juhani Eskola, the director of the Finnish research vaccine program and a new member of the WHO group 'Strategic Advisory Group of Experts' (SAGE), is directly involved with recommending which vaccines—and how many—member countries should purchase for the alleged "pandemic."

According to documents acquired through the Danish Freedom of Information Act, Eskola's Finnish institute, THL, received nearly 6.3 million Euros, ($9,049,760.00), from GlaxoSmithKline (GSK) for "research" on vaccines during 2009.

Not surprising, GlaxoSmithKline produces the H1N1 vaccine ridiculously named 'Pandemrix,' which the Finnish government—following recommendations from Professor Eskola—purchased for their national pandemic reserve stockpiles.

Several other WHO experts also have financial ties to the pharmaceutical industry—a double role that notably has also not been released by the WHO despite their transparency vow.

Primary Source of Income for WHO

The World Health Organization proclaims itself to be an agency that is responsible to provide leadership on global health matters, shaping of the health research agenda, the setting of "norms" and standards, articulation of evidence-based policy options, technical support to countries and the monitoring and assessment of global health trends.

The more than 6.3 million Euros that the WHO's research center received from GlaxoSmithKline represents the WHO vaccine program's number one income source.

And this is on the heels of another dramatic WHO scandal involving Austrian journalist Jane Burgermeister who revealed that the WHO conspired with Baxter International (another vaccine manufacturer) and the United Nations itself to produce and release live bird flu viruses in 2009, all in an effort to trigger the pandemic.

Burgermeister has, in effect, accused the WHO itself [of] planning to commit mass murder.

Scientists on Drug Company Payrolls

As the Flu Case [a website investigating the Burgermeister scandal] articles state, this financial conflict of interest is not an isolated incident with one researcher—the following list of additional WHO researchers, reported to have financial ties to Big Pharma, suggests a more systemic corruption:

- Dr. Peter Figueroa, Professor in the Department of Community Health and Psychiatry in Jamaica, has received money from Merck [a leading drug company].

- Dr. Neil Ferguson has received funding from Baxter, GlaxoSmithKline, and Roche [makers of Tamiflu], as well as from some insurance companies. Professor Malik Peiris in Hong Kong has received money from Baxter, GlaxoSmithKline, and Sanofi Pasteur [a swine flu vaccine maker].

- Dr. Arnold Monto, advisor to Chiron, GlaxoSmithKline, MedImmune, Roche, Novartis, Baxter and Sanofi Pasteur, has received funding from same [all producers of swine flu vaccines or preventive drugs].

- Dr. Friedrich Hayden, consultant to MedImmune and Sanofi Pasteur, received money from those companies, in addition to [drug makers] Roche, RW Johnson, and SmithKlineBeecham.

- And then there is the infamous Dr. Albert Osterhaus, nicknamed "Dr. Flu" because he is head of the European Scientists Fighting Influenza which resides within the WHO structure.

Dr. Osterhaus is a Dutch physician who has been very active in promoting mass vaccination through WHO and the Western media. The government of the Netherlands is currently conducting an emergency investigation into the activities of "Dr. Flu" since it was recently discovered that he had been receiving a salary from several swine flu vaccine companies.

Dr. Osterhaus has received funding from Baxter, Crucell, Novartis, Hoffman-La Roche, MedImmune, Nobilon, Sanofi Pasteur, MSD, GlaxoSmithKline, and Solvay.

Conflicts of Interest

The WHO is in the powerful position of reviewing and making vaccine recommendations to the world. It is disturbing that many of the scientists who sit on various committees of WHO, are presented as 'independent experts', but they carefully conceal the fact that they receive money from pharmaceutical companies.

It is obvious that the WHO is biased in their vaccine recommendations. Normal hygiene measures provide much greater effect than these little-studied and already confirmed as dangerous vaccines. At the same time, WHO refers to the use of masks and hand-washing as a means to combat swine flu only twice in their documents while these erroneous vaccines and other medications are referred to 42 times!

The lack of credible research and clinical study aside, we believe that paid advisers of the pharmaceutical companies should be removed from their positions within the WHO as well as any sovereign government's oversight agency and not be allowed to give recommendations.

Drug Lobbying in Washington, D.C.

The WHO is not unique in its vulnerability to the influence of Big Pharma.

Washington, D.C. is fraught with thousands of industrial lobbyists. They cluster around the band of luxury offices and expensive restaurants that stretch from the White House to the Capitol building—a two-mile axis along which money and power are constantly traded.

No industry wields as much power as the Pharmaceutical Research and Manufacturers Association (PhRMA), a pressure group renowned for its deep pockets and [aggressiveness], even by the standards of U.S. politics.

With the perpetual revolving door between government and the pharmaceutical industry—more and more key government positions are filled with people living "double-lives" with drug/healthcare companies:

President [Barack] Obama's nominee at the Department of Homeland Security overseeing bioterrorism defense, Dr. Tara O'Toole, has served as a key advisor for a lobbying group funded by a pharmaceutical company that has asked the government to spend more money for anthrax vaccines and biodefense research.

Tom Daschle—the former Democratic senator from South Dakota and Senate Majority Leader was President Obama's first pick for secretary of health and human services. Daschle's work included being a paid advisor for a lobbying law firm that earned $16 million representing some of the healthcare industry's most powerful interests. Of course, as you might recall, this nomination didn't fly.

Senior Advisor David Axelrod is accused of collecting big money from Big Pharma to pass healthcare reform by way of his former partners at a Chicago-based firm called AKPD Message and Media. In fact, he founded the firm, and his son is still employed there.

These are but a few examples—many more will be found.

To quote Democratic congressman Sherrod Brown, "PhRMA doesn't need to lobby. The industry is in the White House already."

Bribing Doctors to Prescribe More Drugs

Drug giants not only specialize in influencing government officials, but they also have the ordinary physician in their grips. The practice by drug companies of lavishing gifts upon doctors—far beyond pens and mugs—including exclusive vacations, "consulting" agreements that involve little work and other freebies—is gaining increased scrutiny and disapproval in the public's eye.

Even more quietly, another practice is growing in popularity.

This devious ploy involves private-practice physicians setting up tax-exempt charities, which then receive major donations—to the tune of millions of dollars a year—from drug companies and medical device makers. The "charities" then typically conduct medical research or education, which the physicians behind them promote as being legitimate.

Increasingly, Big Pharma spends billions to influence what doctors see, read and hear, often persuading them to prescribe more drugs, just as it spends billions to taint researchers' decision-making process.

A national survey of physicians published in the *New England Journal of Medicine* in 2007 found that 94 percent of physicians have a "relationship" with the pharmaceutical, medical device, or other related industries.

This massive conflict of interest has prompted Senators Chuck Grassley [of Iowa] and Herb Kohl [of Wisconsin] to introduce a bill called the Physician Payment Sunshine Act, which would require physicians to report annually to the government all payments over $100, beginning in 2010, and that information would be made available to the public. . . .

The Cost of Pushing Pills

Exactly how much does the pharmaceutical industry spend to push their "wonder drugs?"

A study in 2008 attempted to measure those costs, and the results are staggering. They calculated that Big Pharma spends almost twice as much on promotion as they spend on research and development:

The industry spent $57.5 billion on marketing and promotion in 2004 alone far exceeding the $20 billion that was erroneously estimated by the most often quoted research firm, Integrated Medical Systems (IMS).

The amount spent on research and development actually pales in comparison, at $31.5 billion. Add to these figures what the industry also spends in lobbying and it adds up to mind-numbing figures. These numbers clearly demonstrate the need for redirecting the priorities of the industry toward more research, clinical trials and less bribery, pay offs and falsifying marketing.

Until the corrupt ties between Big Pharma and the government [are] cut, healthcare and health policy reform will remain a mere dream. Until then, we can only take what our governments and even our physicians tell us with a grain of salt.

> *"Don't set up a system where saving the world has to be done for profit, then castigate scientists for having to work within it."*

Health Experts Were Not Paid to Hype the H1N1 Threat

Debora MacKenzie

In the following viewpoint, Debora MacKenzie, a science writer for New Scientist *and other journals, refutes the claim that top scientists for the World Health Organization (WHO) were paid by pharmaceutical companies to hype the H1N1 swine flu pandemic. In MacKenzie's opinion, most top scientists rely on funding from big drug companies to do their work and even act as paid consultants at industry conferences. Such scientists would only be acting unscrupulously if they took money to foster a hoax, MacKenzie claims, and that simply was not the case. As MacKenzie asserts, the swine flu did kill people, and the drugs prescribed by health authorities did protect many others from the disease. By alerting the public to the threat, the WHO scientists acted responsibly, MacKenzie argues.*

Debora MacKenzie, "Swine Flu Experts and Big Pharma: No Conspiracy," *New Scientist*, Short Sharp Science blog, June 7, 2010. Reproduced by permission.

As you read, consider the following questions:

1. According to the *BMJ* report cited by MacKenzie, when did WHO officials supposedly begin colluding with drug companies to create profits on flu outbreaks?

2. According to the BMJ piece, what kinds of services did drug companies supposedly pay WHO scientists to perform?

3. What does MacKenzie suggest is the one way to keep scientists from working in the pay of drug companies?

The parade of accusations surrounding the swine flu pandemic continues. The latest, published in the journal *BMJ* [*British Medical Journal*], claims the scientists who advised the World Health Organization (WHO) to declare H1N1 swine flu a pandemic were in the pay of companies that stood to profit from the resulting sales of antiviral drugs and vaccines.

The piece, by Deborah Cohen from *BMJ* and Philip Carter from a privately funded British non-profit called the Bureau for Investigative Journalism, says such conflicts of interest could be handled better. Fair enough, but it also says more: that the scientific advice given to the WHO on flu has been dishonestly slanted since 1999 to profit companies. This would be important if the journalists supported their case. I don't think they do—making this a troubling smear on science.

Scientists Performed Their Proper Duties

In 1999, the WHO started planning global advice on responding to pandemic flu. Cohen and Carter castigate by name scientists who wrote the plans, because at certain times they were also paid to do various jobs by companies that make flu drugs and vaccines.

Sounds wrong, doesn't it? Scientists recommend massive purchases of goods made by companies that pay them. Hard to resist such a great story.

Small problem: this is the only thing they could possibly recommend.

Pandemic flu kills. And there is no way to predict at the outset whether a pandemic will get nasty. So all you can do is start making vaccine and pre-stock antiviral drugs. But surely it matters that these advisers were paid by drug companies? Well, paid to do what? Some, say Cohen and Carter, did research; others were paid speakers at meetings; some merely spoke at a conference a drug company helped support. That last would be hard for any medical researcher to avoid: there are virtually no medical conferences that do not get support from pharma.

But beyond that, top scientific experts on flu drugs and vaccines get that way by doing research on flu drugs and vaccines, and past the basic research stage virtually all of it is paid for by drug companies. Even Cohen and Carter admit that everyone relies on research done by the same pool of scientists.

More Serious Charges Fall Short

So how do you manage all these apparent conflicts? Openness helps—and almost none of this was secret. Cohen and Carter quote scientists cheerfully spelling it all out to them, and saying they signed declarations for the WHO.

The only way any of this can be corrupt is if the scientists taking company money also made recommendations that favoured industry but were scientifically wrong, and it's here the real agenda emerges. Cohen and Carter's piece says the advice to the WHO was wrong. Their allegations are based on charges made in *BMJ* last year [in 2009] that Tamiflu doesn't work, and separate charges that the pandemic was all a hoax to make money for pharma, by Paul Flynn, a British backbench MP [member of Parliament], and Wolfgang Wodarg, a former member of the German parliament, through a committee of the Council of Europe (not, as some mistakenly assume, a European Union body).

None holds any scientific water. Studies showing Tamiflu has marginal effects on mild seasonal flu or its rare bacterial complications have no relevance to Tamiflu's effect in a pandemic, where it was indispensable, as intensive care staff attest.

As for claims that WHO's pandemic response wasted healthcare money, panicked people, and subjected them to "untested" drugs and vaccines—swine flu, by any scientific criteria, was a pandemic, the vaccines were as tested as the regular seasonal vaccines they were based on, Tamiflu worked, and some people, many young and healthy, died.

If this virus had been nastier I bet these same people would have screamed that not enough was done, and blamed that on nefarious company profits too.

Lessons Worth Learning

Ah yes, profit. There are two real problems here. One is readily dealt with. The WHO may well have been clumsy with disclosure rules, especially keeping its emergency pandemic advisers secret. I hope the investigation of its pandemic management now under way will iron that out.

The second is harder. Society—largely through governments' ideological flight from public services in the 1980s—has decreed that the only way to get pandemic drugs and vaccines, at least in Europe and North America, is through private industry. So inevitably industry will profit from a pandemic. And flu scientists will have to work for private companies.

One way to solve this problem would be to de-privatise science done for the public good, as vaccine research was when vaccines were made, until quite recently, by governments. Ironically, some of the scientists castigated by Cohen and Carter for working with industry and government are in fact trying to build the public-private partnerships that might bring that back.

Until that happens, don't set up a system where saving the world has to be done for profit, then castigate scientists for having to work within it.

Periodical and Internet Sources Bibliography

The following articles have been selected to supplement the diverse views presented in this chapter.

Kerry Capell	"How Big Pharma Profits from Swine Flu," *BusinessWeek*, November 25, 2009.
Peter Curson and Alexis Pillsbury	"Swine Flu—the First Pandemic of the 21st Century," *Geodate*, May 2010.
Economist	"Watch Those Pigs!" June 19, 2010.
Cathy Gulli	"Swine Flu Fiasco," *Maclean's*, October 26, 2009.
Debora MacKenzie	"Flu Hoax? Get Real," *New Scientist*, May 22, 2010.
Betsy McKay	"The Flu Season That Fizzled," *Wall Street Journal*, March 2, 2010.
Jim E. Motavalli	"Lessons from Swine Flu," *E: The Environmental Magazine*, May–June 2010.
Michael Specter	"The Fear Factor," *New Yorker*, October 12, 2009.
Steve Sternberg	"Most Americans Immune to Swine Flu," *USA Today*, September 29, 2010.
Arlene Weintraub et al.	"Lessons from the Pandemic That Wasn't," *BusinessWeek*, February 15, 2010.

CHAPTER 3

Are Vaccines Harmful?

Chapter Preface

Vaccination against disease has been part of modern medicine since 1796 when English country doctor Edward Jenner inoculated a young boy with a cowpox serum that proved effective at staving off smallpox, the leading cause of death in the eighteenth-century world. Jenner's celebrity grew, and by the early 1800s, more than a hundred thousand Europeans and Americans had been vaccinated. Throughout the following century, a global campaign for smallpox vaccination led the World Health Assembly (the decision-making body of the UN World Health Organization) to declare in 1980 that the disease had been eradicated from the earth.

Such a success story has convinced many medical professionals to champion the cause of inoculation against the myriad contagions that threaten human health; however, even in Jenner's day, resistance to vaccination was rife. English laws in 1853 and 1867 made vaccination of infants and adolescents compulsory, and some people rejected the notion that the government could mandate such an invasion of privacy. Although the laws stood firm in England, the opposition gained ground in the United States in the late 1800s, repealing compulsory vaccination laws in California, Illinois, West Virginia, and other states. In 1905, however, the US Supreme Court ruled in *Jacobson v. Massachusetts* that obligatory inoculation against smallpox was legal because the duty to protect public welfare outweighed any concerns about personal privacy.

In recent decades, the fight against vaccination has focused in part on the rejection of compulsory-vaccination laws but also on a growing concern that specific vaccines may cause more harm than good. Vaccination has always included a risk that certain members of the inoculated population would have adverse reactions to the vaccine, but the so-called herd immunity approach, which ensures that the majority will be protected, has made the risk acceptable to governmental and health authorities. In the late 1990s, however, a paper published by physician Andrew Wakefield in the British medical journal the *Lancet*, provoked suspicions that the measles, mumps, and rubella (MMR) vaccine was linked to an increased incidence of autism among immunized children. Since then, several celebrities and other notable figures have raised concerns that vaccines may be rushed into service before proper testing periods can guarantee their safe use. In her book *Toxic Overload: A Doctor's Plan for Combating the Illnesses Caused by Chemicals in Our Foods, Our Homes, and Our Medicine Cabinets*, physician Paula Baillie-Hamilton states that "a US study found that children who received vaccines containing a preservative called thimerosal, which is almost 50 percent mercury, were more than twice as likely to develop autism than children who did not." Although other reports refute this claim, thimerosal was voluntarily removed from most childhood vaccines to allay public fears.

In March 2010, a federal court held that thimcrosal is not a cause of autism, a month after the *Lancet* retracted Wakefield's 1998 paper. But the ruling and the retraction have done little to suppress public concerns. In a June 2009 article in *Discover*, writer and blogger Chris Mooney asserts, "The idea that there is something wrong with our vaccines—that they have poisoned a generation of kids, driving an 'epidemic' of autism—continues to be everywhere: on cable news, in celebrity magazines, on blogs, and in health news stories." Mooney argues the continuing resistance comes from parents who feel helpless in explaining their child's autism. He insists that the Internet has given antivaccination groups legitimacy and a platform and that the struggle is now to maintain public confidence in the efficacy of immunization—a struggle that did not occur when smallpox, polio, and other diseases were banished by "wonder drugs" that people overwhelmingly trusted. This contest is apparent in the following chapter, in which authors from diverse backgrounds debate the efficacy and safety of vaccinations as well as the question of whether individuals have the right to opt out of immunization programs.

> "More generally, many of the parents mobilizing against the state policy believe various types of vaccine are being overused, resulting in more cases of autism, attention deficit hyperactivity disorder and other neurological problems in children."

Requiring Mandatory Vaccination Is Dangerous

Associated Press

The Associated Press is an American news agency. In the following viewpoint, parents of preschoolers in New Jersey protest a policy requiring children 6 months to 5 years old attending child-care centers to receive the flu vaccine. Parents in opposition of the state policy believe vaccines are being overused and causing neurological problems in children. Some of the protesters even believe the approach to vaccinations to be "anti-American."

As you read, consider the following questions:

1. According to the article, what types of exemptions to mandatory vaccinations are allowed by the New Jersey state policy?

Associated Press, "Protest over Mandatory Flu Shots for Preschoolers," October 16, 2008. Reproduced by permission.

2. Within the flu vaccine, trace amounts of what substance exists?

3. Why do activists in New Jersey believe that the state "went too far in requiring flu shots"?

As flu season approaches, many New Jersey parents are furious over a first-in-the-nation requirement that children get a flu shot in order to attend preschools and day-care centers. The decision should be the parents', not the state's, they contend.

Hundreds of parents and other activists rallied outside the New Jersey Statehouse on Thursday, decrying the policy and voicing support for a bill that would allow parents to opt out of mandatory vaccinations for their children.

"This is not an anti-vaccine rally—it's a freedom of choice rally," said one of the organizers, Louise Habakus. "This one-size-fits-all approach is really very anti-American."

New Jersey's policy was approved last December by the state's Public Health Council and is taking effect this fall. Children from 6 months to 5 years old who attend a child-care center or preschool have until Dec. 31 to receive the flu vaccine, along with a pneumococcal vaccine.

The Health Council was acting on the recommendations of the federal Centers for Disease Control and Prevention, which has depicted children under 5 as a group particularly in need of flu shots. But no other state has made the shots mandatory for children of any age.

Opposition to Vaccine

"Vaccines not only protect the child being vaccinated but also the general community and the most vulnerable individuals within the community," New Jersey's Health Department said in a statement. It has depicted young children as "particularly efficient" in transmitting the flu to others.

Opposition to the policy is vehement. Assemblywoman Charlotte Vandervalk, one of the speakers at the rally, said she now has 34 co-sponsors for a bill that would allow for conscientious objections to mandatory vaccinations.

"The right to informed consent is so basic," she said in an interview. "Parents have a right to decide for their own children what is injected in their bodies."

State policy now allows for medical and religious exemptions to mandatory vaccinations, but Vandervalk said requests for medical exemptions often have been turned down by local health authorities. She said 19 other states allow conscientious exemptions like those envisioned in her bill.

New Jersey's health department has come out strongly against the legislation.

"Broad exemptions to mandatory vaccination weaken the entire compliance and enforcement structure," it said.

The department also contends that New Jersey is particularly vulnerable to vaccine-preventable diseases—with a high population density, a mobile population and many recently arrived immigrants.

"In light of New Jersey's special traits, the highest number of children possible must receive vaccines to protect them and others," the department said.

Several hundred people attended Thursday's rally, some with signs reading, "Mommy knows best."

Too Many Vaccines

Among the speakers was Robin Stavola of Colts Neck, N.J., who said her daughter, Holly, died in 2000 at age 5 less than two weeks after receiving eight different vaccines, including a booster shot.

"I am not against vaccines, but I do believe there are too many," she told the crowd.

State health officials and the CDC insist the flu vaccine is safe and effective, but Vandervalk and the parent groups who

Vaccines Provoke Unnatural Autoimmune Responses

Naturally acquired immunity by illness evolves by spread of a virus from the respiratory tract to the liver, thymus, spleen, and bone marrow. When symptoms begin, the entire immune response has been mobilized to repel the invading virus. This complex immune system response creates antibodies that confer lifelong immunity against that invading virus and prepares the child to respond promptly to an infection by the same virus in the future.

Vaccination, in contrast, results in the persisting of live virus or other foreign antigens within the cells of the body, a situation that may provoke auto-immune reactions as the body attempts to destroy its own infected cells. There is no surprise that the incidence of auto-immune diseases . . . has risen sharply in this era of multiple vaccine immunization.

James Howenstine,
"Why You Should Avoid Taking Vaccines,"
NewsWithViews.com, December 7, 2003.
www.newswithviews.com.

support her bill contend there has been inadequate research into the vaccine's impact on small children. Critics note that flu vaccines contain trace amounts of thimerosol, a mercury-based preservative; the CDC says there's no convincing evidence these trace amounts cause harm.

More generally, many of the parents mobilizing against the state policy believe various types of vaccine are being overused, resulting in more cases of autism, attention deficit hyperactivity disorder and other neurological problems in children.

"There's not been a response from the government that is credible in terms of doing the scientific research that will screen out vulnerable children," said Barbara Loe Fisher, a speaker at the rally. She is co-founder of the National Vaccine Information Center in Vienna, Va., an advocacy group skeptical of vaccination policies.

"There's an acknowledgment that prescription drugs can cause different reactions in people, but there's a blanket statement by health authorities that we all have to vaccinate, all in the same way," Fisher said.

Fisher is a prominent player in a nationwide movement challenging the scope of vaccination programs. She was harshly critical last year when school officials in Maryland's Prince George's County threatened to impose jail terms and fines on parents whose children didn't get required vaccinations.

The State Went Too Far

Many of the activists in New Jersey accept the need for mandatory vaccinations for certain highly dangerous diseases, such as polio, but argue that the state went too far in requiring flu shots.

"The flu is not a deadly disease," said Barbara Majeski of Princeton, N.J., who does not want her two preschooler sons to get the vaccination.

In fact, flu kills about 36,000 Americans a year and hospitalizes about 200,000. But children make up a small fraction of the victims—86 died last year, from babies to teens, according to federal figures. Only two flu deaths of children in New Jersey have been recorded since 2004.

"Mother Nature designed our bodies to be able to fight off infections through natural means—you need to be exposed and develop immunity," Majeski said. "We've just gotten a little too overprotective with our children."

"The currently available vaccines approved by the FDA are at least a millionfold safer than the infections they are designed to prevent."

Vaccines Are Safe and Effective

Brenda L. Bartlett and Stephen K. Tyring

In the following viewpoint, Brenda L. Bartlett and Stephen K. Tyring argue that vaccines have had very salutary effects on human health, wiping out some diseases and holding others at bay. Although the authors point out the benefits of mandatory vaccinations for whole populations, they focus more on the risks run by those who opt out of vaccine treatments. In some cases, resistance to vaccination has led to the resurgence of formerly controlled diseases, Bartlett and Tyring assert. Thus, they offer examples of currently used vaccines and the positive effects of their widespread implementation. Brenda L. Bartlett is a medical doctor at the Center for Clinical Studies at the University of Texas Health Science Center in Houston. Stephen K. Tyring is a medical doctor in the Department of Pediatrics at the same institution.

Brenda L. Bartlett and Stephen K. Tyring, "Safety and Efficacy of Vaccines," *Dermatologic Therapy*, March/April 2009, pp. 97–103. Reprinted by permission.

As you read, consider the following questions:

1. According to Bartlett and Tyring, what percentage of the 131 documented cases of measles in the United States came from nonvaccinated individuals?

2. What benefits does the Gardasil vaccine have for women, as Bartlett and Tyring report?

3. As the authors state, what is the BCG vaccine used to prevent?

In 1796, [Edward] Jenner started recommending scarification with cowpox as a means of preventing smallpox. This bold suggestion was based on his observations that milkmaids who developed lesions of cowpox on their hands rarely become ill with smallpox. Because the virus to prevent smallpox came from a cow, i.e., *vacca*, the word vaccination was coined. The risk/benefit ratio of vaccination was clear, considering the high rate of morbidity and mortality of smallpox. Eventually, vaccination with cowpox was replaced with vaccinia [virus]. Rarely, a patient would develop eczema vaccinatum, a condition with significant morbidity and a potential for mortality. Considering that smallpox was the deadliest infection in history until its eradication in 1977, the value of vaccination, with very rare exceptions, was beyond question. In fact, the eradication of smallpox using vaccination plus public health measures, e.g., quarantine, is considered by many experts as the most significant breakthrough in medical history. Since then, vaccines have become available for a number of viral and bacterial diseases. Extensive clinical trials precede the approval of vaccines in order to determine their safety and efficacy.

An Important Part of Public Health

Thus far, smallpox is the first and only infectious disease that has been eradicated. The goal that polio would be eradicated by 2005, the 50th anniversary of the first effective vaccine, was not met. The primary reason that polio still kills and cripples children in several countries is not the lack of an effective vaccine but rather ignorance and superstition because of lack of education.

Vaccines should always be used in combination with good public health measures. Such measures could include safer sex, condoms, testing blood products before use, as well as not sharing needles and cocaine straws to prevent transmission of such diseases as hepatitis B and the human immunodeficiency virus (HIV). Proper hand washing prevents transmission of a number of viral and bacterial diseases. Isolation and use of surgical masks are useful to reduce transmission of respiratory infections. Availability of safe drinking water and proper sewage disposal are necessary to prevent enteric infections. Vector control (e.g., mosquitoes) is very important to reduce transmission of one of the world's major causes of death, malaria, as well as a number of viral diseases (e.g., dengue fever, yellow fever, and West Nile fever). Most importantly, education is needed so that the public understands the safety, efficacy and need for available vaccines, and the role of public health measures.

The Risks of Nonvaccination

As a result of widespread use of the measles/mumps/rubella (MMR) vaccine during the past 40 years, these common childhood diseases have become rare in the United States and Europe in the 21st century. These diseases, however, are still very common in other parts of the world. In fact, measles is one of the most contagious diseases known in terms of the number of viral particles needed to produce disease. Until early in the 21st century, over one million children died of measles in the world each year because of lack of access to vaccination, malnutrition, and secondary bacterial infections. Many new parents in the United States and Europe, however, have reached adulthood without ever having known anyone with measles, mumps, or rubella. Therefore, they feel there is no need to vaccinate their children against these diseases. Recent increases in rates of these diseases in the United States are primarily caused by these unvaccinated individuals traveling to international destinations where such infections are common and then returning home with the infection. They subsequently may spread the infection to unvaccinated friends and classmates, which has been the source of several outbreaks in the United States in recent years.

During January–July 2008, 131 measles cases were reported to the Centers for Disease Control and Prevention (CDC) compared with an average of 63 cases per year during 2000–2007. Of the 131 measles cases reported during the first 7 months of 2008, 91% were in unvaccinated individuals or in persons whose vaccination status was unknown. Among the 131 measles cases, 89% were imported from or associated with importations from other countries. These findings document that maintaining high overall MMR vaccination coverage rates is needed to continue to limit the spread of these infections.

In addition to some parents seeing no need for vaccination, there is also the unfounded fear of autism resulting from MMR. The basis of this fear is that MMR is usually given at 1 year of age, but autism is usually not easily diagnosed before 2 years of age. To the lay public, one event preceding another translates to "cause and effect." The alleged link between autism and MMR has led to several independent studies by the Food and Drug Administration (FDA), the CDC, the Institute of Medicine, and the computerized health networks of several European countries. All of these studies, collectively involving tens of thousands of vaccinated children, showed absolutely no causal association between MMR and autism. Despite the data, the National Autism Association, a lay advocacy group, continues to allege that MMR causes autism. In addition, a number of antivaccination web sites express a range of concerns related to vaccine safety and varying levels of distrust in medicine. . . .

The extreme measures to which the vaccine manufacturers must go in order to assure safety is best illustrated by the rotavirus vaccine that was marketed a decade ago. Although rotaviruses kill almost one million children each year and the vaccine was very effective, the rotavirus vaccine was taken off the market due to an increase of eight additional cases of intussusception [where the intestine telescopes in on itself] per million vaccinated children. Despite the fact that the rotavirus vaccine was not proven to cause this surgically correctible condition, the removal of the vaccine from the market put millions of children at risk of contracting this deadly infection. Therefore, the medical/legal issue of "do no harm" took precedence over saving millions of lives. Fortunately, however, two other rotavirus vaccines are now available and are not associated with an increased rate of intussusception.

The Benefits of Gardasil for Women

The two newest vaccines that target infectious diseases with mucocutaneous manifestations are Gardasil and Zostavax, which were both approved by the FDA in 2006. Gardasil is a quadrivalent recombinant vaccine made from viruslike particles based on the L (late) 1 capsid proteins of human papillomavirus (HPV) types 6, 11, 16, and 18. Because the vaccine is recombinant, it has no potential to cause infection. Because HPV types 6 and 11 are responsible for almost all anogenital warts and HPV types 16 and 18 are responsible for approximately 70% of cervical cancers and the majority of external genital cancers, this vaccine has immense potential to reduce morbidity and mortality. This potential is especially significant when one considers that cervical cancer is the number two cancer killer of women in the world. Because several other oncogenic [cancer-causing] HPV types collectively cause the other 30% of cervical cancers, however, women should continue to have regular Pap smears.

Gardasil was originally approved for females aged 9–26 years as a prevention of anogenital warts and cervical cancer, but recently, it was also approved for prevention of vaginal and vulvar cancers caused by HPV types 16 and 18. Although Gardasil is highly effective at preventing a number of benign and malignant lesions, it has no known therapeutic potential. If given to a woman infected with one, two, or three of the four HPV types represented in Gardasil, however, it can protect against the remaining type(s). In addition, up to 40% cross-protection has been demonstrated against oncogenic HPV types closely related to HPV 16 or HPV 18.

Although the duration of protection is still unknown, the primary concern with most potential recipients of the vaccine and/or their parents is safety. Published studies have demonstrated that Gardasil is very safe, but like all studies involving thousands of patients, adverse events were reported. No serious adverse event was observed to be greater in Gardasil recipients than in placebo recipients, but headache, fever, dizziness, and syncope [fainting] have been reported in Gardasil recipients as well as pain on intramuscular injection and erythema [redness] at the injection site.

Although safety and efficacy are always a concern, cost-effectiveness is an important criterion in deciding whether to recommend Gardasil, especially considering that each of the three injections in the series costs approximately $120. A recent study [in the *New England Journal of Medicine*] by [J.J.] Kim and [S.J.] Goldie demonstrated that the greatest cost/benefit ratio was in preadolescent girls, who presumably were not infected with any of the four HPV types represented in the vaccine. In addition, "catch-up" programs aimed at women and girls younger than 21 years of age would also be relatively cost-effective. The cost-effectiveness in these populations, however, is dependent on high levels of vaccine coverage. Al-

The Benefits of Vaccination Outweigh the Risks

To be clear, there is no such thing as a perfectly safe vaccine. Like any other medical treatment, there are side effects and risks involved. In rare cases, live attenuated vaccines could induce the illness they protect against, which could even be spread to those who are not vaccinated. Most of the known risks are rare and relatively minor— most people are familiar with the redness and swelling following a flu shot—and the benefits of vaccination far outweigh them.

Mike Pazos, Science Progress, February 17, 2009.
www.scienceprogress.org.

though the vaccine is currently approved for women up to 26 years of age, there are millions of women older than 26 years at risk of HPV infections. Currently, FDA approval of the vaccine for the latter group of women is pending.

Gardasil's Use in Men

Studies are currently ongoing in males. As in females, there appears to be no significant safety issues with the use of Gardasil in males, and the vaccine is demonstrating the same high rate of efficacy in preventing anogenital warts. In addition, the use of Gardasil in gay men is expected to significantly reduce the rate of anal cancer, which has reached epidemic levels in this population. The vaccine is also expected to have more significant public health implications when given to both sexes because it would prevent infection of males with oncogenic HPV types, thus reducing the chances that these viruses would be passed to female partners. In addition, widespread use of Gardasil may decrease the incidence of certain oral and pharyngeal cancers.

When Gardasil is FDA approved for males, [which it was in October 2009,] it is expected that dermatologists would play an active role in use of this vaccine. Currently, dermatologists should educate their patients about the link between HPV and anogenital cancer and warts. They should remind their HPV-infected male patients about the HPV vaccine (and Pap smears) for their female partners. In addition, dermatologists should identify their female patients at risk for HPV infection and refer them to their gynecologists or pediatricians for consideration of Gardasil vaccination.

A number of questions are still pending regarding the use of Gardasil, one of which is whether receiving Gardasil should be mandatory for preadolescent girls to attend school. Although making Gardasil mandatory for this population would be expected to result in significant reductions in morbidity and mortality from HPV-related diseases and result in marked cost savings, only one state, Virginia, has made this vaccine mandatory. Making the vaccine mandatory would also obligate the state to provide it for those girls who could not afford the high cost of the vaccine, i.e., the same population at greatest risk for cervical cancer. Other vaccines are mandatory, but they are given to both sexes. Making a vaccine mandatory, however, increases compliance severalfold as was seen with Varivax, the vaccine to prevent varicella [chickenpox], now mandatory in most states. One reason some members of the lay public might be against making any vaccine mandatory is based on their misunderstanding of the term. In fact, making a vaccine mandatory simply means that the parents would need to "opt out" of vaccination if they did not want their child to receive the vaccine. If the vaccine was not mandatory, they would need to "opt in." As a result of Gardasil not being mandatory in 49 states, its relatively high cost, and the perception by some individuals that it is a vaccine against a sexually transmitted disease, instead of a vaccine against cancer, only 10% of the eligible females have received Gardasil during the first 2 years since its approval.

A Safe Vaccine for Shingles

The other vaccine of particular interest to dermatologists that was approved in 2006, Zostavax, was studied in 38,546 individuals over age 60 who denied a history of herpes zoster [shingles]. The recipients of the vaccine had a 51% reduction in the incidence of shingles versus the placebo recipients. Among those persons who developed shingles despite receiving Zostavax, there was a 66% reduction in postherpetic neuralgia. Although a 51% reduction in the incidence in shingles is much lower than the reduction in the incidence of diseases prevented by MMR, Gardasil, Varivax, etc., Zostavax is designed to prevent a reemergence of a virus sitting latently in the patient's dorsal root ganglia for years (as opposed to preventing a primary infection).

Considering that Zostavax is a 14-fold concentrated version of Varivax, which has been given to tens of millions of children to prevent primary varicella zoster virus (VZV) infection, it is not surprising that Zostavax has an excellent safety profile. There was no difference between the recipients of Zostavax and placebo in terms of systemic adverse events. Recipients of Zostavax, however, did experience higher rates of local reactions, i.e., erythema, swelling, etc., than did recipients of placebo.

Compliance with the recommendation for Zostavax in persons at least 60 years of age, however, has been very low, i.e., only 2% of eligible persons have received the vaccine. One reason may be that persons in this age group may not remember having had chickenpox and not feel they are at risk for shingles. In addition, many persons do not have insurance plans that cover Zostavax.

It is unlikely that shingles will become a rare disease in the United States as has chickenpox. In addition to the low compliance with its recommended use and its 51% efficacy, its duration of protection is unknown. Although the vaccine is approved for persons at least 60 years of age, the average age of persons who develop shingles is in their sixth decade, i.e., between ages 50 and 60 years. Therefore, most persons who will develop shingles will do so before they are old enough to receive Zostavax. Naturally, anyone under 60 years of age *could* receive Zostavax, but they would need to pay approximately $250 for the vaccine. Studies, however, are ongoing to determine the safety and efficacy of Zostavax in persons between 50 and 60 years of age. It is likely that the FDA will approve Zostavax for persons in this age group.

Because Zostavax is a live attenuated viral vaccine, i.e., Oka strain, it is contraindicated in immunocompromised persons. The number of immunocompromised patients is increasing, which is another reason that shingles in unlikely to become a rare disease. A possible reason that the incidence of shingles may increase before it decreases is the widespread use of Varivax, which has resulted in very few children bringing home wild-type chickenpox to their parents and grandparents. Without the immune boosting of the wild-type virus, more cases of shingles may be seen in younger individuals.

The only reported cases of transmission of the vaccine strain from a recipient of Varivax or Zostavax to a VZV seronegative person have followed the development of a vesicular rash in the recipients of the vaccine. Most recipients, however, do not develop a rash. Therefore, the question remains unanswered whether recipients of either vaccine "shed" Oka strain VZV in their saliva and can transmit the virus to unvaccinated infants or other VZV seronegative individuals via coughing or sneezing.

Preventing Bacterial Infections

Vaccines are available for a number of bacterial diseases, but the need also exists for improved versions of existing vaccines. For example, Bacillus Calmette-Guérin (BCG) vaccination is used in many parts of the world for prevention of tuberculosis, but BCG provides inadequate protection that appears to decline further with time. Because tuberculosis kills over one million persons each year, an improved vaccine is desperately needed. A vaccine is currently available to protect against seven strains of *Streptococcus pneumoniae*, but a new vaccine is pending approval that protects against 13 strains. Available meningococcal vaccines protect against four strains of *Neisseria meningitides*, but vaccines that protect against other deadly strains of this organism are needed. Vaccines are needed against other bacterial and viral diseases, but no vaccines are available against fungal diseases or protozoan diseases, e.g., malaria and leishmaniasis.

New Methods of Vaccine Production

Influenza is a viral disease with rare cutaneous manifestations, but considering its associated morbidity and mortality, it is of concern to all dermatologists and their patients. Until recently, influenza vaccines were all produced in chicken eggs, which was a very inefficient process. First, the strains that were likely to affect the population had to be identified, then the vaccine had to be approved. Millions of chicken eggs must be processed and inoculated and the virus harvested. The virus must then be inactivated and further processed to produce a vaccine. This process was slow and at risk from avian diseases, e.g., avian influenza. More recently, vaccine production has focused on cell culture and recombinant techniques as well as highly innovate methods. For example, one formulation involves vaccine antigens that are produced by combining toll-like receptor-mediated immune enhancers and recombinant bacteria.

Although the first vaccine was given by scarification, most vaccines are given by injection. The first oral vaccine was given to prevent polio, but is no longer in widespread use. Both available vaccines to prevent rotavirus infections, however, are given orally. In addition, one influenza vaccine, Flumist, is given intranasally [as a nasal spray]. A number of vaccines under study have demonstrated efficacy when given topically or intravaginally. It is likely that many future vaccines will be given via nontraditional (i.e., other than injectable) routes.

The Path to Eradicating Diseases

In summary, vaccines have been very successful in preventing morbidity and mortality and, when used in combination with good public health measures, have been the primary reason for significant increases in life spans in many parts of the world. Vaccines are still needed for many infectious diseases. The greatest disappointment in vaccine research thus far in the 21st century is the lack of significant progress toward a vaccine to prevent infection with HIV. Although much hope was placed on the replication-attenuated adenovirus vaccine carrying recombinant *pol*, *nef*, and *gag*, this vaccine, which was safe and immunogenic, did not result in clinical protection against HIV. The currently available vaccines approved by the FDA are at least a millionfold safer than the infections they are designed to prevent, but safety monitoring continues after FDA approval. . . . It is hoped that continued vaccine research will result in other deadly infectious diseases following smallpox down the path to eradication.

> "The number of vaccines given to U.S. kids has expanded dramatically . . . during the exact time period when autism cases have exploded."

Compelling Evidence Shows That Vaccines Trigger Autism

J.B. Handley

J.B. Handley is the founder of Generation Rescue, a nonprofit organization of physicians, researchers, and parents investigating the causes and treatments of autism. Handley claims in the following viewpoint that the high rate of autism among American children has occurred in recent decades when childhood vaccines have also grown in number. Arguing that science has shown the dangers of some vaccines, Handley believes that overdosing children on vaccinations is unwise. He notes that other nations do not prescribe as many vaccinations, and their children do not suffer such high rates of autism. Handley regrets that America has not tempered its immunization schedules as other countries have, but he maintains this probably has to do with the fact that vaccine makers commonly sit on health panels that mandate regular vaccination.

J.B. Handley, "Autism Is Preventable and Reversible," Larry King Live Blogs, April 2009. Reprinted by permission.

As you read, consider the following questions:

1. By what percentage has the number of autistic children in the United States grown since the 1970s, as Handley reports?

2. As Handley explains, how many immunizations does the average American child receive compared with children in the rest of the world?

3. According to the author, countries that give one-third of the number of vaccinations prescribed in the United States report autism rates that are what percentage of American autism rates?

[A]ctress] Jenny McCarthy's son Evan no longer has autism. This is a very hard concept for most people to grasp, because the popular understanding of autism is that it's lifelong. Quietly, a revolution of tens of thousands of parents around the world are standing firmly behind Jenny and using the same treatments to heal their children that she used to heal Evan. Not a day goes by where I don't hear a story from a parent of their child's dramatic improvement or complete recovery from autism using what we call "biomedical intervention."

In the 1940s, autism was supposed to be a placeholder diagnosis, used until we had a better understanding of the actual physical issues that would define autism as a disease. Yet even today, a child is diagnosed based entirely on behavioral observation—there is no blood test or other way to test for it. Unfortunately, this has led to a level of inertia and acceptance amongst the mainstream medical community that many parents find unhelpful, if not unacceptable. "Autism is something you can't really change, just learn to accept it"—that's the message so many of us hear from our medical authorities.

Imagine for a second being that parent of a child with autism and told that your child may never speak and that a lifetime of care is likely. You start to do your own research, and you happen upon our community, filled with hope, examples of recovery, and specific actions you can take to heal your child. What would you do?

Autism and Vaccines

The vaccine issue has made autism one of the most polarizing topics on earth, which is too bad, because it keeps different communities within the autism world from working for the benefit of the only group that matters: our kids.

The number of children diagnosed with autism today is deeply alarming. The 1 in 150 number often used here in the U.S. is actually from 7 years ago [2002], and we're hearing more recent numbers well below 1 in 100 in states like Minnesota, New Jersey, and Oregon, to name just a few. Published studies in the 1970s showed an autism rate of 1 in 10,000, so autism has grown 100-fold, or 10,000%, numbers that are nearly impossible to imagine.

With autism cases growing this quickly, something in the environment has to be causing the rise. A "spontaneous genetic epidemic" is a scientific impossibility. It's also likely that something relatively straightforward has to be behind the epidemic—it's very unlikely that 100 different things all showed up sometime in the early 1990s and triggered the autism epidemic.

That's where vaccines come in, and I think the case for them as a primary trigger is, unfortunately, very compelling. Firstly, the number of vaccines given to U.S. kids has expanded dramatically. Up until 1989, our kids received 10 total shots by their 5th birthday. Today, they receive 36. At their 2 month old appointment alone, most American children receive 6 separate vaccines in less than 15 minutes. Few other things on the planet that nearly all children receive have grown so dramatically during the exact time period when autism cases have exploded.

Known Dangers of Vaccines

Secondly, and this is something most parents don't realize, vaccines are known to cause brain injury in some kids. In fact, the US government has paid out over $1.8 billion in compensation for vaccine injury, most of it to children and much of that for brain injury. How exactly do vaccines cause brain injury? No one knows for sure, but if you check out the Vaccine Injury Compensation Program on the website of the Department of Health and Human Services, you can see for yourself that brain injury is a primary side effect (sometimes called "encephalopathy") of many of our vaccines.

Finally, we have tens of thousands of case reports of parents reporting that their child developmentally regressed, stopped talking, and was later diagnosed with autism after a vaccine appointment. The number of vaccines have risen along with autism rates, vaccines are known to cause brain damage, and parents report regression and later autism after getting them. Is it really so hard to believe we think vaccines are a trigger?

Few parents appreciate that American kids are the most vaccinated on the planet. Generation Rescue just released a study called "Autism and Vaccines Around the World" which will surprise many. We looked at the vaccine schedules of 30 other first world countries to compare how many doses of vaccines children receive. What did we find? Compared to our 36, the average for the rest of the first world is 18, or half of the U.S. schedule. Perhaps more shocking, we looked at countries with the lowest rates of mortality for children under 5 (the U.S. ranks a disappointing 34th, behind Cuba and Slovenia). How many vaccines do the 5 countries with the lowest under 5 mortality rates give? Well, Iceland, Sweden, Singapore, Japan, and Norway give 11, 11, 13, 11, and 13 vaccines respectively—all less than 1/3 the number of vaccines the U.S. mandates!

Why the MMR Vaccine?

How do you say vaccines don't cause autism when only a single vaccine—MMR—has ever been looked at for its relationship to autism? What about the other 10 vaccines our children receive through 36 doses?

Jenny McCarthy, Huffington Post,
March 9, 2010. www.huffingtonpost.com.

How do autism rates compare in some of these other countries? Iceland's rate is 1 in 1,000, Finland's 1 in 700, and Sweden's 1 in 800. These countries give 1/3 the vaccines we do and have autism rates that are as little as one-tenth of ours? Something isn't right.

No Room for Moderation

Parents just want a simple answer: "What do I do for my child? I want to give vaccines, but I don't want autism." There is no perfect answer as our kids are so different. But, perhaps you could start by considering the US vaccine schedule in 1989, which is a schedule many countries still use today. In 1989, we gave the following vaccines (and doses): DTP [diptheria, tetanus, and pertussis] (5), Polio (4), MMR [measles, mumps, and rubella] (1). For reference, today we give the following vaccines and doses: DTP (5), Polio (4), MMR (2), Hepatitis B (3), Hib (4), Varicella (2), Rotavirus (3), PCV [pneumococcal vaccine] (4), Flu (7), Hepatitis A (2).

Prevent deadly disease while preventing autism, why can't the two co-exist?

To date, our health authorities have been unwilling to meet us halfway on vaccines. There appears to be no room for moderation, and we hear the American Academy of Pediatrics state that American children should simply get all their shots. Yet, looking at 30 other first world countries, we found that only 3 others had added Varicella [chickenpox] to their schedules, and only 2 others had added Rotavirus to their schedules, as two examples of low rates of adoption by other countries, despite the fact that both of these vaccines have now been on the market for over a decade. What do these other countries know that we don't? Would it surprise you to learn that the patent holder for Rotavirus sat on the government panel that adds vaccines to our schedule?

Our health authorities are also quick to assert that "the science shows vaccines don't cause autism." It's disappointing to hear false statements like this from people many of us inherently trust. Having read every study these experts put forward, I can tell you with conviction that any doctor making this claim is either lying or has never read the studies for themselves. In fact, we were so frustrated by this mantra about "the science" that we created a website to analyze all the studies, which you can now find at FourteenStudies.org and see for yourself. In a nutshell, if you never look at unvaccinated kids and if you only ever study one vaccine (the MMR) which accounts for 2 of the 36 vaccines our kids get, its easy to craft studies to get the answers you want.

The debate over the causes of autism will not end anytime soon. Parents trying to do the right thing for their children are being put in the middle. I'm grateful for people like Jenny McCarthy who are willing to share their own stories and help as many parents as possible prevent and reverse autism. Through her courage alone, thousands of kids today are facing a far brighter future.

> "We have to move forward and be willing to accept what science tells us: Vaccines do not cause autism."

Vaccines Do Not Cause Autism

Kelley King Heyworth

In the following viewpoint, Kelley King Heyworth reports that the medical community is overwhelmingly supportive of childhood vaccinations. Heyworth believes that despite a growing movement that insists on a causal connection between vaccinations and autism, evidence refutes this claim. As one doctor explains in Heyworth's viewpoint, there is more likely a coincidental link between immunization schedules and diagnoses of autism because the disease tends to arise when children are young— around the same ages that they are receiving vaccinations. Heyworth warns that refusing vaccination for fear of autism endangers the unvaccinated child and the whole community because formerly controlled diseases such as measles and whooping cough have reemerged in unvaccinated populations. Kelley King Heyworth is a writer who has written for Parents *and* Sports Illustrated *magazines. She is married to a medical researcher.*

Kelley King Heyworth, "Vaccines: The Reality Behind the Debate," *Parents*, May 2010. Reprinted by permission.

As you read, consider the following questions:

1. As Heyworth writes, what mercury-containing preservative in vaccines did Andrew Wakefield argue might push infants' mercury exposure beyond safe limits?

2. According to the author, what happened to Wakefield's notorious publication in February 2010?

3. As Heyworth reports, why did the drug manufacturer Merck recall certain lots of the Hib vaccine distributed in 2007?

As Summer Estall approached her first birthday, her mom, Lisa, had more on her mind than party plans. Summer was about to receive not only cake, and presents, but also— surprise!—her fourth round of shots in ten months. "Her last vaccinations had been tough," says Estall, of Grand Forks, North Dakota. "She was her usual happy self after being examined by the doctor, but then we were called into a room where two nurses were both holding long needles. They told me to lay Summer on the table, pull her pants down, and pin down her arms. Of course, she started to scream, and it felt like I was preparing her for torture. By the time the nurses got the Band-Aids on, Summer seemed to be okay—but I was a wreck."

However, it wasn't just the painful pricks that worried Estall about her daughter's 12-month shots. "Everywhere I go, someone's talking about the danger of vaccines," she says. "There are moms posting about their kids' side effects on just about every online parenting forum. The other day I had coffee with two friends, and one of them said she wasn't vaccinating her kids. I can't help but wonder: Should I really be injecting a healthy child with these things?"

Medical Community Supports Vaccination

The answer from the vast majority of medical experts is a resounding "yes." The Centers for Disease Control and Prevention (CDC) and the American Academy of Pediatrics (AAP) recommend that healthy children get vaccinated against 14 diseases by age 2 (with boosters later for some), along with an annual inoculation against the flu. In fact, the government supports vaccines so strongly that any uninsured child can walk into a clinic and get his or her shots for free. "Immunizations are simply one of the greatest public-health achievements," says Mary Glodé, M.D., professor of pediatrics at the University of Colorado in Denver.

And yet, despite doctors' reassurances and mounting evidence that underscores the safety and value of vaccination, many educated, dedicated parents are still wary of vaccines—or passionately opposed to them. Although the national immunization rate has remained stable over the past decade (76 percent of children aged 19 to 35 months were up-to-date on all of their shots in 2008), that's still short of the government's goal of 80 percent. In some pockets of the country, a rising number of parents are delaying shots for their kids or skipping certain ones altogether, citing religious or philosophical exemptions from state laws that require kids to be vaccinated in order to attend school. As a result, there have been recent outbreaks of serious diseases that vaccines had virtually wiped out in the U.S., including measles, mumps, pertussis (whooping cough), and *haemophilus influenzae* type b (Hib), which was once the most common cause of bacterial meningitis in kids under 5.

Infectious-disease specialists say these cases are due to a breakdown of what's known as "herd immunity." In order for a community to be fully protected against a disease, 80 to 90 percent of its population needs to have been vaccinated, says pediatrician Lance Rodewald, M.D., director of the Immunization Services Division of the CDC. Whenever coverage drops significantly below that level, a school, a church, or a neighborhood becomes susceptible to the disease. Babies who aren't old enough to get the shot yet are at the greatest risk of becoming sick.

Most of the recent measles outbreaks have been traced to individuals who visited a country where vaccine-preventable diseases still flourish. "The fact is, all of these diseases still exist—some circulate in this country and others are only a plane ride away." says Dr. Rodewald. "They could easily become widespread again if more people refuse vaccines."

Refuting Autism-Vaccination Link

Ask parents what scares them most about the shots, and you'll likely get one answer: autism. Many people believe that the increased number of vaccines—children now get twice as many as they did in 1980 and can receive up to 20 injections by their first birthday—are to blame for the rise in kids with autism spectrum disorders (ASD). The idea first made headlines in 1998, when Andrew Wakefield, M.D., a British gastroenterologist, published a study of 12 children in *The Lancet* that linked the measles, mumps, and rubella (MMR) combination vaccine with intestinal problems that he believed led to autism. The following year, the AAP issued a warning about thimerosal, the mercury-containing preservative that was found in most vaccines. Though it didn't mention autism specifically, it suggested that the use of vaccines with thimerosal could theoretically push an infant's total exposure of mercury, a neurotoxin, above safe limits, and it recommended that the preservative be removed from shots. The vaccine-autism hypothesis was solidly in the mainstream by the time actress Jenny McCarthy went public with her belief that vaccines caused her son's autism, describing in heartbreaking detail how "the soul left his eyes" on a 2007 segment of the *The Oprah Show*. "It was enough to scare any mother," says Eileen Pike, of West Palm Beach, Florida, who has chosen to delay certain vaccines for her son, now 23 months.

However, at least seven large studies in major medical journals have now found no association between the MMR vaccine and ASD—and this February [2010], *The Lancet* officially retracted Dr. Wakefield's original paper. (Revelations that he had failed to disclose connections to lawyers involved in vaccine litigation also emerged.) In March, the U.S. Court of Federal Claims, Office of Special Masters, a group of judges appointed to handle cases of families who believe immunizations were responsible for their child's autism, ruled that thimerosal in vaccines does not increase the risk of the disorder. (In 2008, a federal judge did award compensation to the family of Hannah Poling, a child with mitochondrial disorder, a rare condition that can show symptoms of autism, which she was diagnosed with shortly after receiving five vaccines.) Several demographic analyses have also found that autism rates continued to rise even after thimerosal was removed from all vaccines except some flu shots.

So why are there so many stories of children developing autism shortly after immunizations—not just in the media, but also in the Vaccine Adverse Event Reporting System, the federally cosponsored program that collects reports of suspected vaccine-related injury or illness? Experts believe that the association is almost certainly coincidental. Children get their first dose of the MMR vaccine at 12 to 15 months, the age at which autism symptoms typically become noticeable, says Paul Offit, M.D., director of the vaccine education center at Children's Hospital of Philadelphia and the author of *Autism's False Profits: Bad Science, Risky Medicine, and the Search for a Cure.* "It's the same reason why there are reports of SIDS [sudden infant death syndrome] deaths after DTaP (diphtheria, tetanus, and pertussis) immunizations," says Dr. Offit. "Infants start the DTaP vaccine between 2 and 6 months, which is the time they're also most likely to die from SIDS." In fact, some autism activists now believe that we should't even do more studies about a possible vaccine connection because they take attention and money away from important research that is investigating other potential causes of the disorder. "We have to move forward and be willing to accept what science tells us: Vaccines do not cause autism," says Alison Singer, president of the Autism Science Foundation and the mother of a child with autism.

Weighing the Risks

That doesn't mean that vaccines aren't capable of causing adverse effects beyond a sore arm and a slight fever. In 1986, the government created the National Vaccine Injury Compensation Program to reimburse families whose children had serious side effects, and it has awarded nearly $2 billion on 2,398 claims. But most doctors say that the odds of experiencing a vaccine-related injury are greatly outweighed by the dangers of catching a vaccine-preventable disease. The measles vaccine, for instance, can cause a temporary reduction in platelets (which control bleeding after an injury) in 1 in 30,000 children, but 1 in 2,000 will die if they get measles itself. The DTaP vaccine can cause seizures or a temporary "shocklike" state in 1 in 14,000 people, and acute encephalitis (brain swelling) in 11 in 1 million. But the diseases it prevents— diphthcria, tetanus, and pertussis—are fatal in 1 in 20 cases, 1 in 10 cases, and 1 in 1,500 cases, respectively.

If the FDA determines that a vaccine poses a real risk to more than a tiny percentage of children, the agency won't let it be used. "Before a new vaccine is approved, it goes through a prospective, placebo-controlled trial involving tens of thousands of children," says Dr. Offit, who was a cocreator of RotaTeq, one of two current rotavirus gastroenteritis vaccines. Once a vaccine is in use, side-effect reports are analyzed by the Vaccine Safety Datalink, a program that collects patient information from managed-care organizations. In 2001, government scientists concluded that Wyeth's Rotashield, an earlier vaccine against rotavirus, could cause one extra case of bowel obstruction for every 10,000 babies who were immunized each year, and they halted its use in the U.S. Sometimes vaccines are pulled from shelves as a precaution: In 2007, certain lots of Merck's Hib vaccine were recalled after the company found bacteria on manufacturing equipment, even though the vaccines themselves tested negative for contamination.

Finding a Middle Ground

Not all parents are reassured by facts like these. After all, most have met a child with autism; probably few have seen one who has crippling polio. Moms want to eliminate even a remote chance that their child will experience side effects from a vaccine, and they may fear that multiple injections could overwhelm the immune system. In fact, a national survey of parents published in *Pediatrics* [in April 2010] (although conducted in 2009, before the retraction of Dr. Wakefield's study), found that 54 percent of parents were concerned about the serious adverse effects of vaccines, and 25 percent believed that some vaccines cause autism.

Enter Robert Sears, M.D., author of *The Vaccine Book: Making the Right Decision for Your Child*. Published in 2007, it includes a different immunization schedule that delays or spaces out several vaccines so that children never receive more than two shots at a time—and it has become a bible for many parents. Dr. Sears says that his main purpose is to make sure that children whose parents would otherwise opt out of immunizations get at least some protection. His top concern is aluminum, an ingredient that is added to half of all vaccines to boost their effectiveness. "Most experts believe the amount of aluminum contained in vaccines is safe, but studies in human infants haven't proven that," says Dr. Sears. "Spacing them out seems like the best way to limit overexposure."

Research has shown, however, that kids are exposed to more aluminum in breast milk or infant formula than through vaccines. And in 2004, The Cochrane Collaboration, an international not-for-profit health-care research organization, analyzed five studies on the effects of aluminum-containing vaccines and concluded that children who receive them are no more likely to experience any serious or long-lasting health problems than those who don't. For parents who are concerned about overburdening their child's immune system with multiple vaccines, Dr. Offit points out that young children are exposed to more antigens—bacteria, viruses, toxins, and other substances that can stimulate disease-fighting antibodies—in a single day of eating, playing and breathing than they are through immunizations.

While popular with some parents, Dr. Sears's alternative schedule has been criticized by the AAP. "Vaccines protect babies' immature immune system," says Margaret Fisher, M.D., a pediatrician at The Children's Hospital at Monmouth Medical Center, in New Jersey, and chair of the AAP section on infectious diseases. "When you delay vaccines, you leave children unprotected against dangerous diseases at the time when they're most vulnerable." In 2008, for example, three of the five kids in Minnesota who developed invasive Hib disease (one of whom died) had parents who'd chosen to postpone vaccination. "People always ask me, 'Which shot can I skip?'" says Dr. Fisher. "Honestly, I can't think of one I'd wait on."

Protecting Children and Community

At the heart of the vaccine debate is the idea that when you immunize your children you don't just protect them—you help shield your entire community. Since some kids can't get certain vaccines because they are allergic to ingredients like eggs, or because they have immune-system deficiencies that prevent vaccines from working (such as those with cancer who are undergoing chemotherapy), many people feel that it's up to healthy children to keep vaccination rates at a level that protects the "herd" as much as possible.

This argument isn't just pitting parents against parents—it's also turning parents against their pediatricians. "Parents often have a hard time reasonably assessing the risks involved because they've never had any experience with many of the diseases that vaccines prevent," says Parents advisor Ari Brown, M.D., a pediatrician in Austin, Texas, and author of *Baby 411*. "But I've seen children with serious cases of measles, mumps, and whooping cough, and I have seen a child die from chicken pox. I promise you that these are diseases you don't want your child to get."

Although some doctors are refusing to take on patients whose families don't plan to immunize, it's important for parents and pediatricians to have respectful conversations. In the end, many doctors say that the strongest statement they can make in favor of vaccinating kids is to point to the family photos on their office walls. "Sometimes the only way that I can get through to nervous parents is by telling them that I don't do anything different for my own two children," says Dr. Brown. "Fortunately, most parents do decide to vaccinate."

That was the case [in 2009] when Lisa Estall overcame her fears and celebrated Summer's first birthday with a round of immunizations. And it was the case when Alison Singer brought her 12-year-old daughter, Jodie, who has autism, in for an H1N1 shot. "Kids were dying all across the country from this flu. Just because my daughter has autism doesn't mean she should be denied a potentially lifesaving vaccine," she says. "On the contrary, I wanted her to be protected."

| "As a population, we are against being forcibly medicated. We value our right to choose what is done to our bodies."

Vaccination Refusal Is a Right to Safeguard Personal Health

Sherri Tenpenny

Lecturer, television talk show host, and doctor of osteopathic medicine, Sherri Tenpenny is the president and medical director of OsteoMed II, a clinic located in the Cleveland, Ohio, area that provides conventional, alternative, and preventive medicine. In the following viewpoint, Tenpenny argues that vaccines pose a serious health threat due to known and unknown side effects. She insists that parents must retain the right to refuse vaccination for their children because the risks of these side effects can be debilitating—often more debilitating than the diseases they are meant to prevent. She contends that if society accepts mandated vaccination, then the people have clearly surrendered their autonomy to the state.

As you read, consider the following questions:

1. How does Tenpenny relate vaccination to bioterrorism?

Sherri Tenpenny, "Vaccinations and the Right to Refuse," NewsWithViews.com, September 2005. Reprinted by permission.

2. According to the author, about how many Americans might contract Guillain-Barré syndrome as a result of flu shots each year?

3. In what ways are children and adults who refuse vaccination being discriminated against, in Tenpenny's view?

By way of introduction, I like to tell people I'm a physician by training and a compulsive researcher by inclination. To be specific, I've invested more than seven-thousand hours investigating the under-reported health hazards associated with vaccinations, along with the attendant ethical and legal issues.

What started as a fairly modest research exercise has turned into a second full-time career. I've discussed vaccination hazards on more than 50 radio and television programs, addressed hundreds of professional, political, and trade groups, produced two informational DVDs, and authored numerous articles for both print publications and Internet sites. In addition, I'm scheduled to produce two books relating to the subject over the next year [2006].

Vaccination Poses Serious Threat

The risk of vaccination must be considered as important—and potentially more serious—than the risk of a childhood disease. Years of experience and thousands of hours of research have led to conclusions that are not uniformly accepted: the importance of legally ensuring vaccine exemptions in each State and the right to refuse Nationally mandated vaccinations.

Vaccination is a procedure and vaccines are medications—and both have risks and side effects which are often ignored by the media and, worse, by many in the medical profession. As a population, we are against being forcibly medicated. We value our right to choose what is done to our bodies.

Humans Are Intrinsically Healthy

Humans are intrinsically healthy and tend to remain so if they are given nutritious, non-GMO [genetically modified organism] foods, fresh air, and clean water. We have been blessed with God-given protective barriers against infectious diseases, including our skin and immune system.

Knowing that these facts are true for all members of the human species, how did we come to embrace the idea that injecting solutions of chemically-treated, inactivated viruses, parts of bacteria, traces of animal tissue and heavy metals, such as mercury and aluminum, was a reasonable strategy for keeping human beings—babies, children and adults—healthy?

If a "dirty bomb" exposed a large segment of US citizens simultaneously to Hepatitis B, Hepatitis A, tetanus, pertussis, diphtheria, Haemophilus influenza B, three strains of polio viruses, 3 strains of influenza viruses, measles, mumps, and rubella viruses, the chickenpox virus, and 7 strains of Streptococcus bacteria, we would declare a national emergency. We would call it an "extreme act of BIOTERRORISM". The public outcry would be so immense our government would act accordingly.

And yet, those are the very organisms that we inject through vaccines into our babies and our small children, with immature, underdeveloped immune systems. Many are given all at the same time. But instead of bioterrorism, we call it "protection." Reflect a moment on that irony.

Blaming Anything but Vaccines

Vaccine injuries are reported to be "rare", but only because very few reactions are "accepted" by the Centers for Disease Control (CDC), the Institute of Medicine (IOM) and the Food and Drug Administration (FDA) as being caused by vaccines. I have frequently said that when a vaccine is given, and a bad reaction occurs, "ANYTHING BUT" the vaccine is "blamed" for the reaction. Here is a direct quote from the 6th edition of *Epidemiology & Prevention of Vaccine-Preventable Diseases* called "The Pink Book", published by the CDC:

> There is no distinct syndrome from vaccine administration, and therefore, many *temporally associated* adverse events probably represent background illness rather than illness caused by the vaccine ... The DTaP [diphtheria, tetanus, and pertussis vaccine] may stimulate or precipitate inevitable symptoms of underlying CNS [central nervous system] disorder, such as seizures, infantile spasms, epilepsy or SIDS [sudden infant death syndrome]. By chance alone, some of these cases will seem to be temporally related to DTaP.;

I have to admit, the first time I read that, I cried. Instead of blaming the vaccine for causing the problem, we blame the children for somehow being defective and the "defect" shows up after we inject them.

No Compensation for Harmful Vaccines

Another example of not blaming the vaccine for a reaction comes directly from the National Vaccine Injury compensation table. Only a handful of injuries are covered by this program [which pays if a listed disorder results from vaccination]; if your injury isn't on the table, you don't qualify for compensation. The government says "there is no proof"—no causal association—that the problem that was experienced, the seizure, for example, was caused by the vaccine.

And timing of the injury is important too. For example, the Injury Compensation Table states that if the baby manifests the symptoms of encephalopathy—or brain swelling—within 3 days of being given a DTaP shot, the injury is probably related to the vaccine. If the complication develops on the 4th day—or the 5th, 6th or 7th day—it is not considered to be "causally related" and the parent is ineligible to apply for compensation.

Sort of like saying the black and blue foot you have today had nothing to do with the frozen turkey you dropped on it

Lawful Vaccine Exemptions

Section 6051 of the California Code states that "[a] pupil with a permanent medical exemption or a personal beliefs exemption to immunization shall be admitted unconditionally." Similar wording appears in most of the state laws allowing a personal belief exemption. These are not whimsical choices on the part of the legislators, the parents, or the doctors who support this right. Parents who vaccinate their children base their decisions on the advice they receive from their pediatricians and the other knowledge they have gathered. Parents who choose to waive vaccinations do so for similarly valid reasons.

Jay Gordon, Michigan Law Review, *2009.*

last week, because the discoloration didn't show up within the time allowed to "prove causation."

Side effects and complications from vaccines are considered inconsequential because their numbers are supposedly "statistically insignificant." This conclusion comes from epidemiological research involving large numbers of participants and has nothing to do with the individual person. Population-based conclusions go against one of the most basic tenants of all of medicine: to treat each person as an individual and believe them when they tell you something went wrong after a vaccine.

A "one in a million" reaction may be rare, but if you are "the one", it is 100% to you.

Serious Side Effects

And even if the one-in-a-million reactions are considered "rare" by the CDC, the health care costs associated with those "rare" reactions are not insignificant. Here's one example.

One recognized complication of the flu shot is a condition called Guillain-Barré Syndrome (GBS). Guillain-Barré is a disorder characterized by progressive paralysis, beginning in the feet and advancing up the body, often causing paralysis of the diaphragm and breathing muscles within a matter of hours or days.

Nearly all patients with GBS are hospitalized because of paralysis. The prognosis of GBS varies. Up to 13 percent die and 20 percent more are left significantly disabled, defined, for these purposes, as unable to work for at least a year.

The CDC reports this side effect to be "rare, perhaps 1 or 2 per million flu shots given." Using the numbers determined from a variety of sources—including medical journals and government documents, it can reasonably be assumed that the flu shot may cause 40 cases of GBS per year.

The Healthcare Cost and Utilization Project (HCUP) database reveals that the average hospital charge per person for GBS is nearly $70,000. Add another $40,000 per person for rehabilitation costs after months of paralysis. Therefore the cost to healthcare for this "rare" complication can be approximated to be at least $4.4 million.

This conservative estimate doesn't include lost wages, reduced standards of living for patients who returned to work but had to take a lower paying job because of their illness. And of course, there is no price tag for the "human cost" of being paralyzed and away from your family for months.

More Costs from Vaccinations

The advantageous cost-benefit relationship is one of the main rationalizations given for supporting the national vaccination program at all levels, infants through the elderly. But has anyone seriously analyzed the cost of caring for vaccine complications?

This example of Guillain-Barré represents the cost of just ONE complication. What if the costs for healthcare from all acknowledged side effects were calculated and added to the cost of the National Vaccination programs? What if we add in the parent-observed complications, such as refractory seizures?

Are we getting our money's worth financially? Are we getting our money's worth in terms of a "healthier" nation?

What about other not-so-obvious costs incurred by vaccine mandates—increased taxes and increased health insurance premiums to pay for the shots? Increased administrative costs to track that they have been given? There are many others, but I'll stop there.

Retaining the Right to Refuse

There are three things to take away from this . . . :

1. Low infection rates and high vaccination rates should not be the cornerstone of our public health policy. Vaccine reactions should not be discounted, whatever their numbers. Further, the true cost-benefit of the vaccination program must be considered, and what has been presented is barely the tip of the iceberg.

2. Parents, and all adults, must retain their right to refuse vaccines. They are not without risk, and those "rare" complications can result in significant costs, both economic and in terms of human life.

3. Children and all adults who refuse to be vaccinated are being discriminated against. They are losing their rights:

   a. Rights and access to a public education.

   b. Rights to access to health care, as doctors discharge them as patients.

   c. Rights to food because often moms on Medicaid are refused food stamps.

These rights—including the right to refuse—must be ensured.

When we give government the power to make medical decisions for us—and force us to vaccinate and medicate our children in the name of "health" and "policy" and for "the greater good" we, in essence, accept that the state owns our bodies, and, apparently, our children.

| "Outbreaks of vaccine-preventable disease often start among persons who refused vaccination."

Vaccination Refusal Endangers Public Health

Saad B. Omer et al.

Saad B. Omer is an assistant professor of global health at Emory University's Rollins School of Public Health. In the following viewpoint, Omer and colleagues use statistical evidence to show that immunization has kept the recurrence of diseases in check and that those who refuse vaccination are increasing the risk of disease outbreaks to themselves and their communities. According to the authors, vaccine refusal is becoming more widespread in America because some state laws are very tolerant of exemption and because more people are becoming less trustful of vaccines. As the author notes, parents are particularly cautious when it comes to the safety of their children, and many have accepted reports that vaccines are more harmful than the diseases they are meant to prevent. Therefore, unvaccinated children are becoming more common and are catching and spreading diseases that were once held at bay. Omer and his coauthors insist that if

Saad B. Omer et al., "Vaccine Refusal, Mandatory Immunization, and the Risks of Vaccine-Preventable Diseases," *New England Journal of Medicine*, May 2009, pp. 1981–988. Reprinted by permission.

the benefits of vaccination are to remain a vital part of society,
then greater efforts will be needed to educate the public about
vaccine safety.

As you read, consider the following questions:

1. According to Omer and colleagues, when was the first
   US vaccination law passed?

2. Based on a study done between 1985 and 1992 cited by
   the authors, how many times greater was the risk of
   contracting measles among vaccine-exempt children as
   compared with nonexempt children?

3. As Omer et al. explain, what do studies reveal about
   general-care physicians who provide care to unvaccinated children?

Vaccines are among the most effective tools available for
preventing infectious diseases and their complications
and sequelae [aftereffects]. High immunization coverage has
resulted in drastic declines in vaccine-preventable diseases,
particularly in many high- and middle-income countries. A
reduction in the incidence of a vaccine-preventable disease often leads to the public perception that the severity of the disease and susceptibility to it have decreased. At the same time,
public concern about real or perceived adverse events associated with vaccines has increased. This heightened level of concern often results in an increase in the number of people refusing vaccines.

In the United States, policy interventions, such as immunization requirements for school entry, have contributed to high
vaccine coverage and record or near-record lows in the levels
of vaccine-preventable diseases. Herd immunity, induced by
high vaccination rates, has played an important role in greatly
reducing or eliminating continual endemic transmission of a
number of diseases, thereby benefiting the community overall
in addition to the individual vaccinated person.

Recent parental concerns about perceived vaccine safety issues, such as a purported association between vaccines and autism, though not supported by a credible body of scientific evidence, have led increasing numbers of parents to refuse or delay vaccination for their children. The primary measure of vaccine refusal in the United States is the proportion of children who are exempted from school immunization requirements for nonmedical reasons. There has been an increase in state-level rates of nonmedical exemptions from immunization requirements. In this article, we review the evidentiary basis for school immunization requirements, explore the determinants of vaccine refusal, and discuss the individual and community risks of vaccine-preventable diseases associated with vaccine refusal.

Evolution of Immunization Requirements

Vaccination was introduced in the United States at the turn of the 19th century. The first U.S. law to require smallpox vaccination was passed soon afterward, in 1809 in Massachusetts, to prevent and control frequent smallpox outbreaks that had substantial health and economic consequences. Subsequently, other states enacted similar legislation. Despite the challenges inherent in establishing a reliable and safe vaccine delivery system, vaccination became widely accepted as an effective tool for preventing smallpox through the middle of the 19th century, and the incidence of smallpox declined between 1802 and 1840. In the 1850s, "irregular physicians, the advocates of unorthodox medical theories," led challenges to vaccination. Vaccine use decreased, and smallpox made a major reappearance in the 1870s. Many states passed new vaccination laws, whereas other states started enforcing existing laws. Increased enforcement of the laws often resulted in increased opposition to vaccination. Several states, including California, Illinois, Indiana, Minnesota, Utah, West Virginia, and Wisconsin, repealed compulsory vaccination laws. Many other states retained them.

In a 1905 landmark case, *Jacobson v. Massachusetts*, which has since served as the foundation for public health laws, the U.S. Supreme Court endorsed the rights of states to pass and enforce compulsory vaccination laws. In 1922, deciding a case filed by a girl excluded from a public school (and later a private school) in San Antonio, Texas, the Supreme Court found school immunization requirements to be constitutional. Since then, courts have been generally supportive of the states' power to enact and implement immunization requirements.

Difficulties with efforts to control measles in the 1960s and 1970s ushered in the modern era of immunization laws in the United States. In 1969, a total of 17 states had laws that required children to be vaccinated against measles before entering school, and 12 states had legally mandated requirements for vaccination against all six diseases for which routine immunization was carried out at the time. During the 1970s, efforts were made to strengthen and strictly enforce immunization laws. During measles outbreaks, some state and local health officials excluded from school those students who did not comply with immunization requirements, resulting in minimal backlash, quick improvement in local coverage, and control of outbreaks. Efforts by the public health community and other immunization advocates to increase measles vaccine coverage among school-age children resulted in enforcement of immunization requirements for all vaccines and the introduction of such requirements in states that did not already have them. By the beginning of the 1980s, all 50 states had school immunization requirements.

Recent School Immunization Requirements

Because laws concerning immunization are state-based, there are substantial differences in requirements across the country. The requirements from state to state differ in terms of the school grades covered, the vaccines included, the processes and authority used to introduce new vaccines, reasons for exemptions (medical reasons, religious reasons, philosophical or personal beliefs), and the procedures for granting exemptions.

State immunization laws contain provisions for certain exemptions. As of March 2008, all states permitted medical exemptions from school immunization requirements, 48 states allowed religious exemptions, and 21 states allowed exemptions based on philosophical or personal beliefs. Several states (New York, Arkansas, and Texas) have recently expanded eligibility for exemptions.

Secular and Geographic Trends

Between 1991 and 2004, the mean state-level rate of nonmedical exemptions increased from 0.98 to 1.48%. The increase in exemption rates was not uniform. Exemption rates for states that allowed only religious exemptions remained at approximately 1% between 1991 and 2004; however, in states that allowed exemptions for philosophical or personal beliefs, the mean exemption rate increased from 0.99 to 2.54%.

Like any average, the mean exemption rate presents only part of the picture, since geographic clustering of nonmedical exemptions can result in local accumulation of a critical mass of susceptible children that increases the risk of outbreaks. There is evidence of substantial geographic heterogeneity in nonmedical-exemption rates between and within states. For example, in the period from 2006 through 2007, the state-level nonmedical-exemption rate in Washington was 6%; however, the county-level rate ranged from 1.2 to 26.9%. In a spatial analysis of Michigan's exemption data according to census tracts, 23 statistically significant clusters of increased exemptions were identified. Similar heterogeneity in exemption rates has been identified in Oregon and California (unpublished data).

The reasons for the geographic clustering of exemptions from school vaccination requirements are not fully understood, but they may include characteristics of the local population (e.g., cultural issues, socioeconomic status, or educational level), the beliefs of local health care providers and opinion leaders (e.g., clergy and politicians), and local media coverage. The factors known to be associated with exemption rates are heterogeneity in school policies and the beliefs of school personnel who are responsible for compliance with the immunization requirements.

Instead of refusing vaccines, some parents delay vaccination of their children. Many parents follow novel vaccine schedules proposed by individual physicians (rather than those developed by expert committees with members representing multiple disciplines). Most novel schedules involve administering vaccines over a longer period than that recommended by the Advisory Committee on Immunization Practices and the American Academy of Pediatrics or skipping the administration of some vaccines.

Individual Risk and Vaccine Refusal

Children with nonmedical exemptions are at increased risk for acquiring and transmitting vaccine-preventable diseases. In a retrospective cohort study based on nationwide surveillance data from 1985 through 1992, children with exemptions were 35 times as likely to contract measles as nonexempt children (relative risk, 35; 95% confidence interval [or CI, a statistical interval used to show how likely a given parameter is to be found in a given population], 34 to 37). In a retrospective cohort study in Colorado based on data for the years 1987 through 1998, children with exemptions, as compared with unvaccinated children, were 22 times as likely to have had measles (relative risk, 22.2; 95% CI, 15.9 to 31.1) and almost six times as likely to have had pertussis (relative risk, 5.9; 95% CI, 4.2 to 8.2). Earlier data showed that lower incidences of measles and mumps were associated with the existence and enforcement of immunization requirements for school entry.

The consequences of delayed vaccination, as compared with vaccine refusal, have not been studied in detail. However, it is known that the risk of vaccine-preventable diseases and the risk of sequelae from vaccine-preventable diseases are not constant throughout childhood. Young children are often at increased risk for illness and death related to infectious diseases, and vaccine delays may leave them vulnerable at ages with a high risk of contracting several vaccine-preventable diseases. Moreover, novel vaccine schedules that recommend administering vaccines over a longer period may exacerbate health inequities, since parents with high socioeconomic status are more likely to make the extra visits required under the alternative schedules than parents with low socioeconomic status.

Clustering of Refusals and Risk

Multiple studies have shown an increase in the local risk of vaccine-preventable diseases when there is geographic aggregation of persons refusing vaccination. In Michigan, significant overlap between geographic clusters of nonmedical exemptions and pertussis clusters was documented. The odds ratio for the likelihood that a census tract included in a pertussis cluster would also be included in an exemptions cluster was 2.7 (95% CI, 2.5 to 3.6) after adjustment for demographic factors.

In Colorado, the county-level incidence of measles and pertussis in vaccinated children from 1987 through 1998 was associated with the frequency of exemptions in that county. At least 11% of the nonexempt children who acquired measles were infected through contact with an exempt child. Moreover, school-based outbreaks in Colorado have been associated with increased exemption rates; the mean exemption rate among schools with outbreaks was 4.3%, as compared with 1.5% for the schools that did not have an outbreak (P=0.001 [i.e., a probability value indicating that the outbreaks cannot be ascribed to chance alone]).

High vaccine coverage, particularly at the community level, is extremely important for children who cannot be vaccinated, including children who have medical contraindications to vaccination and those who are too young to be vaccinated. These groups are often more susceptible to the complications of infectious diseases than the general population of children and depend on the protection provided by the vaccination of children in their environs.

Vaccine Refusal and Measles

Measles vaccination has been extremely successful in controlling a disease that previously contributed to considerable morbidity and mortality. In the United States, the reported number of cases dropped from an average of 500,000 annually in the era before vaccination (with reported cases considered to be a fraction of the estimated total, which was more than 2 million) to a mean of 62 cases per year from 2000 through 2007. Between January 1, 2008, and April 25, 2008, there were five measles outbreaks and a total of 64 cases reported. All but one of the persons with measles were either unvaccinated or did not have evidence of immunization. Of the 21 cases among children and adolescents in the vaccine-eligible age group (16 months to 19 years) with a known reason for nonvaccination, 14, or 67%, had obtained a nonmedical exemption and all of the 10 school-age children had obtained a nonmedical exemption. Thirteen cases occurred in children too young to be vaccinated, and in more than a third of the cases (18 of 44) occurring in a known transmission setting the disease was acquired in a health care facility.

Outbreaks of vaccine-preventable disease often start among persons who refused vaccination, spread rapidly within unvaccinated populations, and also spread to other subpopulations. For example, of the four outbreaks with discrete index cases (one outbreak occurred by means of multiple importations) reported January through April 2008, three out of four index cases occurred in people who had refused vaccination due to personal beliefs; vaccination status could not be verified for the remaining cases. In Washington State, a recent outbreak of measles occurred between April 12, 2008, and May 30, 2008, involving 19 cases. All of the persons with measles were unimmunized with the exception of the last case, a person who had been vaccinated. Of the other 18 cases, 1 was an infant who was too young to be vaccinated, 2 were younger than 4 years of age, and the remaining 15 were of school age (unpublished data).

Who Refuses Vaccines and Why

Using data from the National Immunization Survey for the period from 1995 through 2001, [P.J.] Smith et al. compared the characteristics of children between the ages of 19 and 35 months who did not receive any vaccine (unvaccinated) with the characteristics of those who were partially vaccinated (undervaccinated). As compared with the undervaccinated children, the unvaccinated children were more likely to be male, to be white, to belong to households with higher income, to have a married mother with a college education, and to live with four or more children. Other studies have shown that children who are unvaccinated are likely to belong to families that intentionally refuse vaccines, whereas children who are under-vaccinated are likely to have missed some vaccinations because of factors related to the health care system or sociodemographic characteristics.

In a case–control study of the knowledge, attitudes, and beliefs of parents of exempt children as compared with parents of vaccinated children, respondents rated their views of their children's vulnerability to specific diseases, the severity of these diseases, and the efficacy and safety of the specific vaccines available for them. Composite scores were created on the basis of these vaccine-specific responses. As compared with parents of vaccinated children, significantly more parents of exempt children thought their children had a low susceptibility to the diseases (58% vs. 15%, P<0.05), that the severity of the diseases was low (51% vs. 18%, P<0.05), and that the efficacy and safety of the vaccines was low (54% vs. 17% for efficacy and 60% vs. 15% for safety, P<0.05 for both comparisons). Moreover, parents of exempt children were more likely than parents of vaccinated children both to have providers who offered complementary or alternative health care and to obtain information from the Internet and groups opposed to aspects of immunization. The most frequent reason for non-vaccination, stated by 69% of the parents, was concern that the vaccine might cause harm.

Other studies have also reported the importance of parents' concerns about vaccine safety when they decide against vaccination. A national survey of parents from 2001 through 2002 showed that although only 1% of respondents thought vaccines were unsafe, the children of these parents were almost three times as likely to not be up to date on recommended vaccinations as the children of parents who thought that vaccines were safe. In a separate case–control study with a national sample, underimmunization was associated with negative perceptions of vaccine safety (odds ratio, 2.0; 95% CI, 1.2 to 3.4). And in another case–control study, [Jean] Bardenheier et al. found that although concerns regarding general vaccine safety did not differ between the parents of vaccinated children and the parents of undervaccinated or unvaccinated children, more than half of the case and control parents did express concerns about vaccine safety to their child's health care provider. Moreover, parents of undervaccinated or unvaccinated children were more likely to believe that children receive too many vaccines.

The Role of Health Care Providers

Clinicians and other health care providers play a crucial role in parental decision making with regard to immunization.

Health care providers are cited by parents, including parents of unvaccinated children, as the most frequent source of information about vaccination.

In a study of the knowledge, attitudes, and practices of primary care providers, a high proportion of those providing care for children whose parents have refused vaccination and those providing care for appropriately vaccinated children were both found to have favorable opinions of vaccines. However, those providing care for unvaccinated children were less likely to have confidence in vaccine safety (odds ratio, 0.37; 95% CI, 0.19 to 0.72) and less likely to perceive vaccines as benefitting individuals and communities. Moreover, there was overlap between clinicians' unfavorable opinions of vaccines and the likelihood that they had unvaccinated children in their practice.

There is evidence that health care providers have a positive overall effect on parents' decision making with regard to vaccination of their children. In a study by Smith et al., parents who reported that their immunization decisions were influenced by their child's health care provider were almost twice as likely to consider vaccines safe as parents who said their decisions were not influenced by the provider.

In focus-group discussions, several parents who were not certain about vaccinating their child were willing to discuss their immunization concerns with a health care provider and wanted the provider to offer information relevant to their specific concerns. These findings highlight the critical role that clinicians can play in explaining the benefits of immunization and addressing parental concerns about its risks.

Doctors' Response to Refusal

Some clinicians have discontinued or have considered discontinuing their provider relationship with families that refuse vaccines. In a national survey of members of the American Academy of Pediatrics, almost 40% of respondents said they would not provide care to a family that refused all vaccines, and 28% said they would not provide care to a family that refused some vaccines.

The academy's Committee on Bioethics advises against discontinuing care for families that decline vaccines and has recommended that pediatricians "share honestly what is and is not known about the risks and benefits of the vaccine in question." The committee also recommends that clinicians address vaccine refusal by respectfully listening to parental concerns, explaining the risk of nonimmunization, and discussing the specific vaccines that are of most concern to parents. The committee advises against more serious action in a majority of cases: "Continued refusal after adequate discussion should be respected unless the child is put at significant risk of serious harm (e.g., as might be the case during an epidemic). Only then should state agencies be involved to override parental discretion on the basis of medical neglect."

Policy-Level Determinants

Immunization requirements and the policies that ensure compliance with the requirements vary considerably among the states; these variations have been associated with state-level exemption rates. For example, the complexity of procedures for obtaining exemption has been shown to be inversely associated with rates of exemption. Moreover, between 1991 and 2004, the mean annual incidence of pertussis was almost twice as high in states with administrative procedures that made it easy to obtain exemptions as in states that made it difficult.

One possible way to balance individual rights and the greater public good with respect to vaccination would be to institute and broaden administrative controls. For example, a model law proposed for Arkansas suggested that parents seeking nonmedical exemptions be provided with counseling on the hazards of refusing vaccination.

States also differ in terms of meeting the recommendations for age-appropriate coverage for children younger than 2 years of age. School immunization requirements ensure completion by the time of school entry, but they do not directly influence the timeliness of vaccination among preschoolers. However, there is some evidence that school immunization laws have an indirect effect on preschool vaccine coverage. For example, varicella vaccine was introduced in the United States in 1995 and has played an important role in reducing the incidence of chickenpox. In 2000, states that had implemented mandatory immunization for varicella by the time of school entry had coverage among children 19 to 35 months old that was higher than the average for all states. Having an immunization requirement could be an indicator of the effectiveness of a state's immunization program, but the effect of school-based requirements on coverage among preschoolers cannot be completely discounted.

Refusals Increase Risks for All

Vaccine refusal not only increases the individual risk of disease but also increases the risk for the whole community. As a result of substantial gains in reducing vaccine-preventable diseases, the memory of several infectious diseases has faded from the public consciousness and the risk-benefit calculus seems to have shifted in favor of the perceived risks of vaccination in some parents' minds. Major reasons for vaccine refusal in the United States are parental perceptions and concerns about vaccine safety and a low level of concern about the risk of many vaccine-preventable diseases. If the enormous benefits to society from vaccination are to be maintained, increased efforts will be needed to educate the public about those benefits and to increase public confidence in the systems we use to monitor and ensure vaccine safety. Since clinicians have an influence on parental decision making, it is important that they understand the benefits and risks of vaccines and anticipate questions that parents may have about safety. There are a number of sources of information on vaccines that should be useful to both clinicians and parents (e.g., Appendix 1 in the fifth edition of *Vaccines*, edited by [S.] Plotkin et al.; the list of Web sites on vaccine safety posted on the World Health Organization's Web site; and the Web site of the National Center for Immunization and Respiratory Diseases).

Periodical and Internet Sources Bibliography

The following articles have been selected to supplement the diverse views presented in this chapter.

Sharon Begley and Jeneen Interlandi	"Anatomy of a Scare," *Newsweek*, March 2, 2009.
Neil Genzlinger	"Vaccinations: A Hot Debate Still Burning," *New York Times*, April 27, 2010.
Andrew Grant	"Vaccine Phobia Becomes a Public-Health Threat," *Discover*, January/February 2010.
Harriet Hall	"Vaccines and Autism," *Skeptic*, June 3, 2009.
Claudia Kalb	"Stomping Through a Medical Minefield," *Newsweek*, November 3, 2008.
Deborah Kotz	"A Closer Look at Vaccines," *U.S. News & World Report*, February 2009.
Chris Mooney	"Vaccination Nation," *Discover*, June 2009.
Alice Park	"How Safe Are Vaccines?" *Time*, June 2, 2008.
Joel Stein	"The Vaccination War," *Time*, September 28, 2009.
Elizabeth Weise	"Doctors: Letting Kids 'Get' the Flu Is Not a Good Idea," *USA Today*, October 21, 2009.
Keith J. Winstein	"Fear of Vaccines Spurs Outbreaks, Study Says," *Wall Street Journal*, May 7, 2009.

OPPOSING
VIEWPOINTS®
SERIES

CHAPTER 4

Are America and the World Prepared for Coming Pandemics?

Chapter Preface

In 2005, as a response to avian flu outbreaks, the US Home-land Security Council issued preparedness plans for influ-enza pandemics. These measures required that state and local authorities draft plans for dealing with pandemic flu and urged private businesses to create their own response strate-gies to help control the spread of contagions. The council's plans also promised federal involvement including leveraging international partnerships to battle severe outbreaks. Accord-ing to Jeffrey Levi, the executive director of the Trust for America's Health, these preparations paid off. In an April 28, 2009, opinion piece from the *Washington Post* website, Levi re-marked, "There have been significant improvements in sur-veillance, coordination, communications, treatment capabili-ties and stockpiles, vaccine manufacturing capacity, and ensuring that every state now has a pandemic plan." In Levi's view, this strategy helped the US government and local com-munities to quickly respond to the H1N1 swine flu pandemic of that year. Indeed, the government posted updated, relevant information for citizens on its Flu.gov website, and a spate of hand sanitizers appeared in government buildings, schools, and businesses across the country.

Despite the plethora of information and antisepsis, critics argued that the nation was not ready to battle a serious influ-enza pandemic. Back in January 2009, the US House of Rep-resentatives Committee on Homeland Security posted its re-port "Getting Beyond Getting Ready for Pandemic Influenza" that claimed the preparations outlined by the Homeland Se-curity Council had not been fulfilled. According to this report, the federal government had failed to create a unified biosur-veillance strategy, had not coordinated efforts with state or lo-cal government or business leaders, and had ultimately aban-doned its responsibility. In a statement issued just after the report's release, council chairman Bennie G. Thompson of Massachusetts asserted, "Pandemic influenza could destroy the security of our nation and homeland. Yet despite the horrific consequences, we still are not prepared as a nation to fully withstand the impact of such a devastating widespread biological event."

Once the swine flu hit the United States, other critics exposed what they saw as flaws in the system. Government Accountability Office representative Bernice Steinhardt told Reuters news service in June 2009 that US agencies had not tested any plans to allow employees to work at home to avoid sickness, and some segments—such as air traffic controllers—had no option but to remain in confined workspaces where illness could spread quickly. David Harrison, writing for the state policy news service Stateline.org, said in an October 1 post that budget cuts had reduced state health response measures and limited stockpiles of antiviral medications. As Harrison reported, "National pandemic plans suggest stockpiling enough antivirals to treat 25 percent of the population. But 13 states do not have enough antivirals to cover 20 percent of their population." In addition, Harrison noted that states also reported that hospital services and available beds would be swamped if any significant percentage of their populations became ill from a pandemic flu.

Ultimately, the swine flu pandemic did not test the limits of America's preparedness. The expected casualties never materialized, and the outbreak proved far milder than seasonal flu; however, forecasters warn that future pandemics may be more virulent and deadly. The authors in the following chapter debate whether the United States and the world at large are ready for the challenges of a devastating pandemic.

| *"If our pandemic preparedness were to undergo a stress test today, it would fail."*

Federal and State Authorities Are Not Prepared for a Serious Pandemic

Stephen E. Flynn and Irwin Redlener

In the following viewpoint, Stephen E. Flynn and Irwin Redlener warn that the government, health officials, and American public are unprepared for severe epidemics. Using the H1N1 swine flu as an example, the authors claim that if this pandemic had become as virulent as expected, US health facilities would be overwhelmed and the public—caught without personal emergency plans or stores of supplies—would have panicked. Flynn and Redlener believe America must use the time before a more serious disease strikes to train health staffs, stockpile vaccines, and make sure there are no roadblocks to helping the sick. They also assert that the government must keep the public informed of epidemics so that families and individuals can prepare for disaster. Stephen E. Flynn is a homeland security expert at the Council of Foreign Relations and the author of The Edge of Disaster: Rebuilding a Resilient Nation. *Irwin Redlener is the director of the*

Stephen Flynn and Irwin Redlener, "Get Ready for Pandemic," AC360° CNN, May 2009. Reprinted by permission.

National Center for Disaster Preparedness at the Columbia University Mailman School of Public Health and the author of Americans at Risk: Why We Are Not Prepared for Megadisasters and What We Can Do Now.

As you read, consider the following questions:

1. Why do Flynn and Redlener claim that America has been "living on borrowed time" regarding epidemic diseases?

2. According to the US Department of Health and Human Services, as cited by the authors, about how many Americans could become ill if a full-strength pandemic hit the nation?

3. What federal organization do Flynn and Redlener believe might be helpful in distributing vaccines nation-wide during an emergency pandemic?

We may have dodged a bullet—for now. If the strain of Swine Flu virus that is currently [in 2009] circulating the United States remains mild, our plans and capabilities for responding to a nationwide health care crisis will not be put to the test. That is a good thing because if our pandemic preparedness were to undergo a stress test today, it would fail.

A Measured Response

Because panic can lead to misdirected energies that result in harmful outcomes, the [Barack] Obama Administration and local leaders like New York's mayor Michael Bloomberg deserve high marks for providing a measured and reassuring tone in the face of the initial fear and uncertainty surrounding the H1N1 outbreak.

But now the hard work must begin.

President Obama needs to quickly seize upon this crisis to mobilize state and local governments and everyday Americans to better prepare our hospitals, communities, and homes for the task of protecting and saving lives during a virulent pandemic.

The sobering reality is that we have been living on borrowed time. Lethal, new, non-seasonal influenza outbreaks typically strike three to four times a century and we are overdue.

The H1N1 virus has all the microbial evolutionary attributes for producing our millennium's first deadly pandemic: it is a new virus compounded from several distinct strains for which people have no natural immunity; it is transmissible among humans; and, it has caused fatalities in unexpected age groups.

The relatively mild form of the virus we are seeing now could mutate in the upcoming flu season in the southern hemisphere. Then we could see it back in our own communities next winter in a more virulent form.

Overwhelming America's Health Services

According to the U.S. Department of Health and Human Services, full-blown pandemic would result in approximately 90 million Americans becoming ill, and depending on the flu's potency, with anywhere from 865,000 to 9,900,000 requiring hospitalization. To put that number into context, consider that the entire inventory of staffed hospital beds within the United States is 970,000 and virtually all of them are currently occupied.

We are simply not prepared for this kind of outbreak:

- The emergency health care system is incapable of managing the surge of millions of "worried-well" and sick.

- Most of our communities do not have tested plans for the timely distribution of antivirals, vaccines, or protective equipment.

- Within many state and local jurisdictions, confusion remains over who will be in charge during a major medical emergency.

- There is no consistency among states on vaccine prioritization or the best infection-control policies.

- At the family level, too few of us have drawn up emergency plans or stocked up on essential supplies at our homes.

In short, our national leaders would be doing us a disservice if they fail to channel the recent public anxiety over Mexican Swine flu into a national campaign to improve our preparedness.

Monitor Disease and Prepare Health Workers

Here is what needs be done right away:

- The federal government should survey states and localities and make emergency funding available to restore staffing at public health departments. Our first line of defense is the disease surveillance, reporting, and contingency planning these public health officials provide. On the current perilous trajectory, the public health workforce is projected to be 9 percent smaller than in 2005 when the pandemic flu risk first started generating serious concern.

- Hospitals with state and local government support need to have plans and incentives in place to make sure the health care workforce is adequately trained and available to help during a major infectious disease outbreak. Every hand will count, especially since we are already experiencing a nationwide shortage of approximately 100,000 nurses. An April 2009 report of an AFL-CIO [American Federation of Labor–Congress of Industrial

Early Warning System for Disease Outbreaks Needs Strengthening

The current state of disease surveillance by public health and health care delivery organizations does not allow for adequate early warning. There are different thresholds for reporting (meaning that different organizations define how many cases compose an outbreak in their opinion). Additionally, health care professionals receive varying amounts of training regarding the need and process for reporting. Poor initial reporting of cases of Severe Acute Respiratory Syndrome (SARS) in 2002 and 2003 exemplifies this problem. . . . Although avian influenza is worrisome due to its mortality rate (greater than 60% as of September 2008), and is currently moving slowly across the globe, should a new pandemic variant arise with different characteristics (allowing for faster transmission rates, among other things) it will be necessary to have adequate biosurveillance already in place to allow for the earliest warning possible. Waiting for high numbers of people to become ill or worse, die—is unacceptable.

US House Committee on Homeland Security,
January 2009.

Organizations] survey of 104 health care facilities in 14 states reinforced the findings of earlier studies that many medical professionals and workers may not show up for work during a disease outbreak. The reasons include the need to stay at home to provide childcare during school closures or attending to sick loved ones. Equally worrisome, the AFL-CIO survey found that only 43 percent of the facilities have provided pandemic flu training to their employees.

- Managing a lethal pandemic will require innovative action to meet the surge in demand for medical care, including setting up temporary triage centers outside hospitals and using alternative care sites. These auxiliary facilities will be needed to separate the "worried-well" from the truly sick, and to provide spill-over space to isolate those with contagious disease from other bed-ridden patients. The alternative of having an estimated 45 million Americans seeking emergency outpatient services during a pandemic will not work. Today, more than half the nation's 4,000 emergency rooms are operating at or over capacity. One reason why the emergency care system is under such stress is that it has become the only medical care option for the nearly 50 million unfortunate Americans who do not possess health insurance. The severe recession is making this situation worse.

Clear Away Bureaucratic Obstacles

- The federal government needs to provide states with firm guidelines, matched with funding support, and work to resolve the liability issues associated with using locations like conference centers and hotels as temporary mass emergency facilities.

- To help deal with expected staffing shortfalls, Washington also needs to work with state governments to quickly adopt pre-credentialing systems and to clear away the legal barriers so qualified volunteers can help out during a public health emergency.

- Over the next three months, distribution plans must be tested nationwide at the community level to ensure that vaccines or antiviral medicines such as Tamiflu and Relenza can reach an at-risk or infected population in time to be effective. Antivirals need to be taken no later than 48-hours after the appearance of flu symptoms, with some experts suggesting that a 24-hour window would be far better. Our large national stockpile of drugs will be of no help if communities don't have the means in place to rapidly distribute them. One good idea is to turn to the U.S. Postal Service for help, but first we need to make sure that the mail carriers receive training and have early access to antiviral drugs and protective gear.

Help Charities and Inform the Public

- Organizations like the American Red Cross that play such an important support role during times of disasters need a helping hand by corporate and individual donors. Like many charitable organizations, the Red Cross has seen recent and dramatic drops in giving, forcing them to make significant staff reductions.

- Finally and most importantly, as individuals we need to take responsibility for keeping ourselves informed about what we can do to stay healthy during a disease outbreak. We also need to make ourselves more self-reliant. Families should have in place a family emergency plan to include storing a supply of food, medicines, facemasks, and alcohol-based hand rubs. Whether healthy or sick, we might have to confine ourselves to our homes for several days while a pandemic plays itself out.

- By skillfully managing the risk communications associated with the Mexican Swine Flu pandemic, the Obama Administration has earned public credibility for dealing with a national medical emergency. This asset now must be invested into providing the galvanizing leadership the nation requires to think creatively and to act quickly on correcting our dangerous deficit in national pandemic preparedness.

"*More work may need to be done to understand the basis of [antivaccination] beliefs and to address them in the case of a serious influenza outbreak.*"

Americans' Concerns About Vaccination Must Be Overcome to Prepare for Future Pandemics

Gillian K. SteelFisher et al.

In the viewpoint that follows, Gillian K. SteelFisher and her colleagues claim that a significant percentage of Americans avoided vaccination against H1N1 swine flu because of concerns about vaccine safety and a belief that the risk of catching a severe case of the flu was not pressing. SteelFisher, the assistant director of the research program at the Harvard School of Public Health, and her coauthors contend that such fears will need to be allayed or overcome if the government and health officials expect to mount a more successful campaign against more virulent influenza outbreaks in the future.

Gillian K. SteelFisher et al., "The Public's Response to the 2009 H1N1 Influenza Pandemic," *New England Journal of Medicine*, May 19, 2010. Reprinted by permission.

As you read, consider the following questions:

1. In the few months leading up to the release of the H1N1 vaccine, what percent of Americans told pollsters that they expected to be vaccinated, according to the authors?

2. As SteelFisher and her colleagues state, of the parents who said they would not or might not allow their children to be vaccinated, about what percentage based their refusal on the risk that the vaccine might cause another serious illness?

3. According to the authors, what were the two particular concerns that most poll respondents had about the government's reaction to the H1N1 outbreak?

In April 2009, a novel influenza A (H1N1) virus emerged in the United States with the key characteristics of a pandemic virus, and within weeks it had spread to every region in the country.[1] Ultimately, the rate of death was lower than was initially predicted, but the numbers of H1N1 cases, hospitalizations, and deaths were nonetheless substantial,[2] and the experience offers some lessons that may help us to prepare for future influenza outbreaks.

Given the crucial role that the public plays in containing or spreading illness and in seeking related medical care, we have examined the public's response to the 2009 H1N1 pandemic and relevant public health recommendations through a comprehensive review of available data from national public opinion polls conducted by telephone between April 2009 and January 2010. Our sources include 20 polls, 8 of which were conducted by the Harvard School of Public Health (HSPH) through cooperative agreements with the Centers for Disease Control and Prevention (CDC), the National Preparedness Leadership Initiative, and the National Public Health Information Coalition. We examined the extent to which people adopted specific behaviors during three periods: the early months of the pandemic, when no vaccine was available; at the time of the initial, delayed release of vaccine to high-priority groups; and after the vaccine was widely available. We also examined the reasons why many Americans did not get vaccinated and reviewed the public's view of the government's response to the pandemic. In instances in which multiple polling questions were relevant, we present a range of findings.

The Public's Initial Response

Early in the pandemic, when no vaccine was available, a majority of Americans were quick to adopt two central public health recommendations (see Table 1). In the pandemic's first weeks, almost two thirds of Americans (59 to 67%) said that they or someone in their family had begun to wash their hands or clean them with sanitizer more frequently, and a majority (55%) had made preparations to stay at home if they or a family member got sick. It was also recommended that people avoid exposure to others with influenza-like symptoms, and 35 to 38% said they had done that (HSPH, April, May, and June 2009).

Measures for reducing interactions with other people were not recommended as routine practice. Nonetheless, polls suggest that 16 to 25% of Americans had avoided "places where many people are gathered, like sporting events, malls, or public transportation," and 20% had "reduced contact with people outside [their] household as much as possible." Fewer had adopted related measures. For example, 4 to 8% said they or family members had worn a face mask, and 1 to 3% got a prescription for or purchased antiviral drugs (HSPH, April, May, and June 2009).

The Risk of Vaccination

Between July, when discussions about vaccine availability increased, and October, when a limited amount of vaccine became available, the public was divided over whether they would get vaccinated. Roughly half (46 to 57%) of the public said they expected to receive the vaccine (AP, July, September, and October 2009; Fox, September 2009; HSPH, August–September and September 2009; CBS, October 2009); a higher percentage of parents—59 to 70%—said they expected to get their children vaccinated (CBS, August and October 2009; HSPH, September 2009).

In making their decision, some people appeared to think there was a trade-off between accepting the perceived risk associated with the illness and accepting any perceived risk associated with the vaccine. Sixty percent of adults who initially said they did not intend to get the vaccine for themselves and parents who initially said they did not intend to get the vaccine for their children also said that they would change their mind if "there were people in [their] community who were sick or dying from influenza A (H1N1)" (HSPH, September 2009).

There were two major reasons why people said they would not or might not get the H1N1 vaccine, one of which was concern about its safety. Among adults overall, this concern was present but not dominant: most (87%) believed the H1N1 influenza vaccine was "very safe" or "somewhat safe." However, only 33% believed it was "very safe," as compared with 57% who said the same of the seasonal influenza vaccine (HSPH, September 2009). Among adults who said they would not or might not get the H1N1 vaccine, concerns about getting H1N1 influenza, another serious illness, or other side effects from it were top "major reasons" for their decision (cited by 21%, 20%, and 30%, respectively) (see Table 2). Parents who said they would not or might not have their children vaccinated were even more concerned about safety: 33% cited concern about exposure to another serious illness from the vaccine. Furthermore, a higher percentage of these parents than of adults overall indicated that they did not trust public health officials to provide correct information about the vaccine's safety (31% vs. 19%; HSPH, September 2009).

The other major reason for avoiding the H1N1 vaccine was the belief that it was not needed. Among adults overall, 47 to 50% said they were not concerned that they or their family members would get sick with H1N1 in the next 12 months (HSPH, August–September and September 2009). Among adults who said they would not or might not get the vaccine, the second and third most commonly reported reasons were a belief that they were not at risk for getting a serious case of H1N1 infection (28%) and the idea that if they did acquire H1N1, they could get medication to treat it (26%). A similar fraction (27%) of parents who said they would not or might not have their child vaccinated said that they did not think their child was at risk for getting a serious case (HSPH, September 2009).

High-Risk Groups Received Vaccine First

During October, a limited amount of H1N1 influenza vaccine became available and was generally earmarked for high-priority groups, as defined by the CDC's Advisory Committee on Immunization Practices.[3] By early November, 17% of adults had tried to get the vaccine for themselves, but 7 in 10 (70%) were unable to get it, so only 5 to 6% had been vaccinated (HSPH, October–November 2009; Gallup and AP, November 2009). Among high-priority adults, one in five (21%) tried to get the vaccine, but two thirds (66%) of them were unable to get it. Thus, only 7% of high-priority adults were actually vaccinated (HSPH, October–November 2009). Children, who were also prioritized, had higher vaccination rates than adults. Roughly 4 in 10 parents (41%) tried to get the vaccine for their children, and two thirds (66%) were unable to do so, meaning that 14 to 17% of parents had their children vaccinated (HSPH, October–November 2009; Gallup and AP, November 2009). Among people who tried and failed to get the vaccine, more than half (55%) said they were frustrated, but 91% said they would try again (HSPH, October–November 2009).

The vaccine was released more widely in mid-December, at the same time that concern about getting sick with H1N1 declined: the proportion of people who were concerned about getting sick had dropped from the peak of between 51 and 59% in October and November (AP, October 2009; Marist, October 2009; AP, November 2009) to 40% by mid-December (HSPH, December 2009). At that time, 14% of adults had received the vaccine. Seventeen percent and 21% had received it by early and mid-January, respectively, in a poll in which adults were defined as 19 years of age or older[4] (HSPH, January 2010). In mid-January, an additional 16% said they intended to get it "by the end of February 2010." Substantially fewer adults had received the vaccine by mid-January than had expressed interest in receiving it when asked during the period from July through October.

Safety Concerns Kept Many Away

A substantially greater proportion of parents had gotten the vaccine for their children than did adults for themselves: 35% of parents had had one or more of their children vaccinated by mid-December, and 40% had done so by mid-January. In addition, 13% of parents said they intended to have children vaccinated "by the end of February 2010" (HSPH, December 2009 and January 2010). In total, 29% of those 6 months to 19 years of age had received the vaccine.[4]

During the December–January period, a belief that the vaccine was not safe or that it was not needed continued to be a major factor in the decisions of adults who said they were not going to or might not get the vaccine. Parents who said they were not going to or might not get the vaccine for their children were even more likely than the parallel group of adults to cite safety concerns as a reason (56% vs. 35%; HSPH, January 2010).

Table 1: Behavioral Response to 2009 H1N1 Influenza During the Early Months of the Pandemic*

Behavior	April 2009	May 2009	June 2009
		% of respondents	
Initial recommendation			
Wash your hands or use hand sanitizer more frequently	59	67	62
Make preparations to stay at home if you or a family member are sick	Not asked	55	Not asked
Take steps to avoid being near someone with flulike symptoms†	Not asked	35	38
Interaction with others			
Avoid places where many people are gathered together, such as sporting events, malls, or public transportation‡∫	25	25	16
Avoid people you think may have recently visited Mexico	20	16	Not asked
Avoid Mexican restaurants or grocery stores	17	13	Not asked
Reduce contact with people outside your own household as much as possible	Not asked	Not asked	20
Avoid large shopping areas or malls	Not asked	Not asked	14
Avoid air travel∫	Not asked	27	13
Limit your use of public transportation, buses, and trains	Not asked	Not asked	12
Reduce your attendance at church, temple, mosque, or other place of worship	Not asked	Not asked	6
Avoid family or personal events, such as parties, wedding ceremonies, or funeral services	Not asked	Not asked	6
Physical contact with others during interaction			
Stop shaking hands with people†	Not asked	14	12
Stop hugging and kissing close friends or relatives†	Not asked	12	9
Wear a face mask	8	4	6
Contact with health professionals			
Talk with your doctor about health issues related to H1N1 or swine flu	5	8	Not asked
Get a prescription for or purchase an antiviral drug, such as Tamiflu or Relenza	1	2	3

* Data are from Harvard School of Public Health polls, April, May, and June 2009.
† The language in this question focused on "you personally" rather than on "you or anyone in your household."
‡ The June 28, 2009, poll did not include "or public transportation."
∫ In April and May polls, respondents were provided with "yes" or "no" response options for this question. In June, respondents were given an additional explicit category of "No one in your household did this before the outbreak."

Table 2: Major Reasons Respondents Said They Would Not or Might Not Get the 2009 H1N1 Influenza Vaccine*

Reason	Adults Not Getting Vaccine for Themselves	Parents Not Getting Vaccine for Their Children
	% of respondents	
September 2009		
Concern about other side effects from the vaccine	30	38
Doubt about the risk of getting a serious case	28	27
Belief that it is possible to get medication to treat H1N1	26	NA
Concern about getting H1N1 from the vaccine	21	24
Concern about getting another serious illness from the vaccine	20	33†
Concern that vaccine is too expensive	20	13
Distrust that public health officials would provide correct information about vaccine safety	19	31†
Doubt about the vaccine's effectiveness	17	23
Dislike of injections	16	15
Plan to get seasonal flu vaccine and belief that it would protect against H1N1	14	12
Recommendation from a health care provider not to be vaccinated	10	7
Difficulty in getting to a vaccination site	8	4
Age of a child under 6 months (ineligible for vaccine)	NA	3
January 2010		
Doubt that outbreak is as serious as public officials once thought	37	32
Concern about safety risks from the vaccine	35	56†
Doubt about the risk of getting a serious case	30‡	20
Belief that it is possible to get medication to treat H1N1	27	33
Belief that it is too late in the flu season to make getting the vaccine worthwhile	11	11
Previous infection with H1N1	8	14†

* Data are from Harvard School of Public Health polls, September 2009 and January 2010.
† The proportion of parents choosing this reason was significantly higher than the proportion of adults responding to the question about getting the vaccine for themselves (P<0.05).
‡ The proportion of adults choosing this reason was significantly higher than the proportion of parents responding to the question about getting the vaccine for their children (P<0.05).

TAKEN FROM: Gillian K. Steel Fisher, "The Public's Response to the 2009 H1N1 Influenza Pandemic," *New England Journal of Medicine*, May 19, 2010. www.nejm.org.

By December, a quarter (24%) of adults had talked to a doctor or other health care professional about getting the H1N1 vaccine for themselves, and of those, 53% said the practitioner had recommended getting the vaccine, 17% said that the practitioner had recommended against it, and 30% said that the practitioner had made no recommendation either way. More than a third (37%) of parents talked to a doctor or other health care professional about getting the H1N1 vaccine for their child, and of those, two thirds (64%) said that the practitioner had recommended getting the vaccine, 10% said that the practitioner had recommended against it, and 25% said that the practitioner had made no recommendation (HSPH, December 2009).

Complaints Against the Government

Throughout the H1N1 pandemic, more than half the U.S. population appeared to have a positive impression of the government's response, although a sizable minority did not. For example, in the early days of the pandemic, 54% believed the response of the federal government was appropriate, whereas 39% believed the government had overreacted (CNN, May 2009). Nine months later, in January 2010, 59% believed that public health officials did an excellent or good job in their overall response to the pandemic, whereas 39% believed they did a fair or poor job (HSPH, January 2010).

The public expressed two particular concerns about the government's response. First, some people were displeased with the vaccine shortage, and while the shortage existed, a majority of respondents (54%) said the federal government was doing a poor or very poor job of providing the country with adequate vaccine supplies (Gallup). Second, the public was divided about public health officials' efforts to make sure the H1N1 vaccine was safe early in the distribution process, even though two thirds (63%) of the public said in January that "public health officials had done the right amount to make sure the H1N1 flu vaccine is safe" (HSPH, January 2009). For example, in November, adults were nearly evenly divided on whether medical testing of the H1N1 influenza vaccine had moved too quickly to ensure that it was safe: 45% said it was done as quickly as possible while still making sure the vaccine was safe, whereas 40% said it was done too quickly so that people could not be sure it was safe (Fox, November 2009).

Allaying Public Distrust and Skepticism

Our review of these data suggests that in the event of a future influenza pandemic, a substantial proportion of the public may not take a newly developed vaccine because they may believe that the illness does not pose a serious health threat, because they (especially parents) may be concerned about the safety of the available vaccine, or both. More work may need to be done to understand the basis of these beliefs and to address them in the case of a serious influenza outbreak.

Polls during the 2009 H1N1 pandemic also suggest that public health communication efforts related to other personal influenza-prevention behaviors were effective in reaching a large swath of the public. Building on these efforts, as well as developing a vaccine strategy, may be useful during response planning and during an outbreak.

Notes

1. H1N1: meeting the challenge. Washington, DC: Department of Health and Human Services. (Accessed May 17, 2010, at http://www.flu.gov/timeline.)
2. CDC estimates of 2009 H1N1 cases, hospitalizations and deaths in the United States, April 2009–March 13, 2010. Atlanta: Centers for Disease Control and Prevention, April 2010. (Accessed May 17, 2010, at http://www.cdc.gov/h1n1flu/estimates_2009_h1n1.htm#Table%20Cumulative.)

3. *Idem.* 2009 H1N1 vaccination recommendations. Atlanta: Centers for Disease Control and Prevention, October 15, 2009. (Accessed May 13, 2010, at http://www.cdc.gov/h1n1flu/vaccination/acip.htm.)

4. Interim results: influenza A (H1N1) 2009 monovalent vaccination coverage—United States, October–December 2009. MMWR Morb Mortal Wkly Rep 2010;59:44–8. (Also available at http://www.cdc.gov/mmwr/pdf/wk/mm59e0115.pdf.)

| "The immediacy and potentially strate-
gic significance of the bioweapons
threat is not widely appreciated, nor is
the country prepared to cope with the
consequences of major bioattacks."

America Is Not Prepared for Bioterrorism Attacks

Tara O'Toole

*Tara O'Toole is undersecretary for science and technology at the
Department of Homeland Security. At the time she gave the congressional testimony from which the following viewpoint was
taken, she was serving as the director of the Center for Biosecu-
rity at the University of Pittsburgh Medical Center. O'Toole here
argues that the United States is not prepared to meet a bioterrorism threat. O'Toole maintains that even after the September
11 terrorist attacks and the anthrax scare of 2001, the government has not taken necessary measures to strengthen US defenses. In fact, as O'Toole reports, government funding for biose-
curity has been cut, leaving defenses stripped of vital personnel
and technology. Furthermore, she asserts that the health services
have no adequate plans for mass sickness due to bioterrorism,
nor does the medical infrastructure have enough diagnostic*

Tara O'Toole, Testimony Before the US Senate Committee on Homeland Security and
Governmental Affairs, October 23, 2007. Reprinted by permission.

equipment or vaccines to treat victims of biological weapons. Finally, O'Toole insists that the Bio Watch system—set up in 2003 to monitor airborne toxins in major cities—needs reconsideration as part of America's frontline defense because of its inability to cut down on response times from detection to reaction and because of its expense.

As you read, consider the following questions:

1. Who does O'Toole say would not likely have "even a rudimentary situational awareness" during a bioterrorism attack?

2. As the author reports, the Department of Health and Human Services requested in 2002 that 75 million doses of anthrax vaccine be manufactured. How long after that request did a company finally get awarded the contract to manufacture the vaccine?

3. According to O'Toole, about how many years behind the rest of the economy is the health industry in terms of digitalizing its business and clinical files?

Six years after anthrax was mailed to members of the U.S. Congress and to media organizations [in 2001], the immediacy and potentially strategic significance of the bioweapons threat is not widely appreciated, nor is the country prepared to cope with the consequences of major bioattacks. This is the case in spite of the extensive efforts to improve U.S. biodefense capabilities, including important contributions by this committee [the Senate Committee on Homeland Security and Governmental Affairs], to catalyze and oversee the agencies and programs involved in the response to large-scale bioattacks and pandemics.

An Urgent Threat

A June 2001 report by the Defense Science Board noted that there are no technical barriers to large-scale bioattacks.

... Major impediments to the development of biological weapons—strain availability, weaponization technology, and delivery technology—have been largely eliminated in the last decade by rapid, global spread of biotechnology.

—Defense Science Board,
Biological Defense, June 2001; p. 18.

Dozens of government and technical reports released since 9/11 and the October 2001 anthrax mailings have affirmed the viability of terrorist groups wielding biological weapons that could cause death, suffering, and social and economic disruption on a calamitous scale. The National Academy of Sciences has published at least a dozen reports on bioterrorism in the past six years.

The [2005] Robb-Silverman Report on WMD [weapons of mass destruction] Intelligence Capabilities documented that "al Qaeda [the terrorist group responsible for the 9/11 attacks] had a major bioweapons effort [in Afghanistan]" as of 2003. We do not know what became of this program, but we do know that al Qaeda representatives have asserted their right to kill up to four million Americans and issued a 2003 fatwa [Islamic decree] authorizing the use of biological, chemical, and nuclear weapons against non-Muslims, and we know that al Qaeda in Iraq has called for scientists to join the jihad [holy war] for the purpose of producing "WMD." Almost two years ago the National Intelligence Council noted that:

Our greatest concern is that terrorists might acquire biological agents, or less likely, a nuclear device, either of which could cause mass casualties.

—National Intelligence Council 2020 Project,
Mapping the Global Future, January 2005.

More recently, analysts in and out of government have written that al Qaeda has regrouped to become "stronger and more resilient" and presents a greater threat to the U.S. than at any time since before 9/11. Key judgments of a July 2007 National Intelligence Estimate include the assessment that:

... al-Qa'ida will continue to try to acquire and employ chemical, biological, radiological or nuclear material in attacks and would not hesitate to use them ...

Yet, in spite of all these sobering reports and expert findings, progress in preparing the country to mitigate the consequences of a bioattack has been slow and modest. There have been accomplishments to be sure, thanks in large part to highly skilled civil servants in federal and state governments who have worked long hours—some almost continuously since 9/11—to fund, staff, and manage vital biodefense programs. . . .

United States Lacks Biodefense

But it is highly disturbing that six years after the 2001 attacks, and in the face of continuous documentation of the seriousness of the biothreat, we face the following realities:

- There is no conduct of operations plan to guide national or local response to an anthrax attack.

- The country has inadequate supplies of anthrax vaccine stockpiled; it would require years at present production capacity to produce enough to immunize the military or the civilian population.

- Only a handful of cities or states could distribute materials from the SNS [Strategic National Stockpile] in a timely manner.

- The country is unprepared to cope with the medical demands of a mass casualty event.

- There are no approved, point-of-care diagnostic tests that physicians could use to diagnose (and rule out) anthrax or any other bioterror threat agent—this is critical in a context of scarce, potentially life-saving resources.

- Should there be a covert biological attack on U.S. civilians, it is highly unlikely that the national command structure, or governors, or mayors would have even rudimentary situational awareness during a bioattack.

As we have learned, building an effective civilian biodefense capability is a much larger and more difficult proposition than was recognized in 2001. The scale of our ambitions and the level of federal funding have not been equal to the challenges we face. The level of leadership attention—in both the executive and legislative branches, and at both the federal and state levels—has been inadequate.

Last week [in October 2007], the White House released Homeland Security Presidential Directive 21, establishing a national strategy for public health and medical preparedness for catastrophic events. This document, which reflects a wealth of input from medical and public health practitioners and experts in disaster response, begins to display the extent and complexity of what it will take to construct a robust biodefense. Creating a homeland defense that secures the country against devastating bioattacks will be the work of a generation. If we do it correctly, we will create the capacity to eliminate bioweapons as agents of mass lethality and take a major national security threat off the table. Moreover, if we approach this vital defense strategy with imagination and vision, we could greatly relieve the suffering and premature death from naturally occurring infectious disease in the U.S. and globally.

Holes in the BioShield

In 2002, it was officially determined that anthrax attacks represented a "material threat" to the U.S. HHS [Department of Health and Human Services] then established a requirement for 75 million doses of "second generation" anthrax vaccine to be delivered in 2008. It was not until two years after HHS determined that it needed such a countermeasure that the contract to produce this vaccine was awarded. Four years later, in

December 2006, HHS canceled the contract, reportedly because of FDA [Food and Drug Administration] concerns about the vaccine's stability. It took HHS another nine months to conclude a contract to acquire 18.75 million doses of the original, "first generation" anthrax vaccine. So, instead of anticipating delivery of second generation anthrax vaccine next year, the country is starting over in its quest for such vaccine. We currently have enough first generation anthrax vaccine in the stockpile to immunize about three million people—not enough to immunize a single, large city.

How did we get to this point? There is a broad consensus among representatives of the biopharma industry and outside observers as to what is wrong with the BioShield program, created in 2004 to allow development and acquisition of essential medical countermeasures for the Strategic National Stockpile (SNS), and how to fix it. The problems and proposed solutions were well documented in the record leading up to the 2006 passage of the Pandemic and All-Hazards Preparedness Act [PAHPA]. The critical problems with BioShield are these:

Insufficient Money for Critical Biodefense Countermeasures

There is not enough money in the BioShield Special Reserve Fund to cover the costs of developing and purchasing even the most high-priority countermeasures. HHS has operated under the assumption that it must satisfy the requirements for all countermeasures for all credible CBRN [chemical, biological, radiological, and nuclear] threats—not just biothreats—with the $5.6 billion fund appropriated in 2004. (Approximately $3.6 billion remains.) When one considers that the average cost of drug development is $800 million—and this is before a single pill or vaccine is purchased—it is obvious that $5.6 billion is not sufficient to protect the nation against the range of potential biothreats, let alone chemical, radiological, or nuclear threats. . . .

Moreover, medical countermeasures degrade over time—they have shelf lives and must be renewed periodically. The traditional approach to vaccine and drug manufacture is to build facilities dedicated to the production of a single product. FDA licensure is linked to approval of manufacturing processes in a particular plant for a particular product. For many of the products in the SNS—anthrax vaccine for example—the government is the only customer. Thus, maintaining the manufacturing capacity to ensure periodic refreshment of the SNS requires maintaining a "warm base"—an entire manufacturing plant that exists only to supply the U.S. government's needs. This is an expensive proposition.

Flawed Contracting Processes

The result of all this is that HHS has taken a long time to make decisions. The mean time from HHS' receipt of a Material Threat Determination to RFP [request for proposal, to initiate the contract process with a manufacturer] to BioShield award is 27 months. This long delay is at odds with the business realities of the biopharma business. Small biotech companies, in particular, are unable to wait this long for decisions. These timeframes have seriously eroded the willingness of companies and of private capital to participate in biodefense work. If HHS does not soon exhibit a more aggressive determination to pursue success, fewer and fewer companies will agree to participate, and HHS's investment choices will wither. Furthermore, such delays in the contracting process translate into long gaps of years during which essential countermeasures are unavailable. . . .

BARDA, the Biodefense Advanced Research and Development Authority written into the PAHPA legislation, is seen by most observers and by industry as key to BioShield's success, and passage of the bill in December 2006 was seen as a signal of the government's ongoing commitment to biodefense. BARDA was intended to improve coordination of BioShield activities across government agencies and to bridge the gap between early stage basic research and drug target "discovery" and late-stage product development and procurement. This gap, encompassing advanced development and clinical testing activities, is sometimes referred to as the "valley of death" because drug and vaccine development is so difficult, time consuming and risky. Smaller companies are at high risk of going under during this period.

Congress authorized $1.07 billion for BARDA in FY [fiscal year] 06–08—this was seen at the time as the start of what would be needed to accomplish BARDA's long-term goals. However, no money was appropriated for BARDA in FY06, and only $99 million was given to BARDA in the FY07 supplemental appropriation. The Administration has requested $189 million for BARDA in FY08. Both the House and Senate versions of the Labor-HHS appropriations bills contain less than the President's request ($135.5 million is proposed in the House, while the Senate version contains $159 million). It is important to understand that biotech and pharmaceutical companies read these relatively small numbers as evidence that the U.S. Congress is not serious about biodefense and does not intend to invest in the development of medicines and vaccines against bioterror threats. Are these companies wrong?

Coordinating Agencies

Biodefense programs within the DHS [Department of Homeland Security] Directorate of Science and Technology have become more coherent and mature over time, thanks in part to the dedication and leadership of Undersecretary [Jay M.] Cohen and Dr. John Vitko. BioWatch technologies have improved since they were first deployed and some serious operational flaws have been addressed. . . .

There has been a strong federal focus on surveillance initiatives designed to detect bioattacks or natural epidemics.

The Government Has Failed to Grasp the Threat of Bioterrorism

A revolution in biotechnology continues, expanding potentially dangerous dual-use capabilities across the globe. As the delayed response to H1N1 has demonstrated, the United States is woefully behind in its capability to rapidly produce vaccines and therapeutics, essential steps for adequately responding to a biological threat, whether natural or man-made.

H1N1 came with months of warning. But even with time to prepare, the epidemic peaked before most Americans had access to vaccine. A bioattack will come with no such warning. Response is a complex series of links in a chain of resilience necessary to protect the United States from biological attacks. Rapid detection and diagnosis capabilities are the first links, followed by providing actionable information to federal, state, and local leaders and the general public; having adequate supplies of appropriate medical countermeasures; quickly distributing those countermeasures; treating and isolating the sick in medical facilities; protecting the well through vaccines and prophylactic medications; and in certain cases, such as anthrax, environmental cleanup. We conclude that virtually all links are weak, and require the highest priority of attention from the Administration and Congress.

US Commission on the Prevention of Weapons of Mass Destruction Proliferation and Terrorism, January 2010.

This is a desirable goal—it is one of the holy grails of public health—but it is very difficult to achieve. Now, after six years of significant federal and state investment in a range of environmental sensor systems, syndromic surveillance, and a panoply of local attempts to build surveillance systems of all types, it is a good time to stand back and examine the nation's overall surveillance strategy. There is a need for a longer-term strategy that balances investments in detection against the need to ensure situational awareness during an event; that ensures collaboration between DHS and the various agencies within HHS that deal with aspects of surveillance; and that ensures better coordination between federal and local efforts. There is also a pressing need to consider the long-term maintenance costs of these programs, which can be considerable.

In my view, we have not paid sufficient attention to the need to provide decision makers at all levels with adequate situational awareness during a public health disaster. This is a major strategic issue, and it is not clear who in government, or even which agency, "owns" it. There is, I believe, a mistaken assumption that a great deal of health data will be available— for example, the number of people who are ill or admitted to hospitals with certain diagnoses or the availability and locale of critical resources such as available hospital beds, equipment, drugs, etc. But the healthcare industry is a decade behind the rest of the economy in digitalizing its business functions and the clinical side of health care. Thus, there are likely to be dangerous delays in gathering the basic information that will be needed to manage the crisis. It may well be that rapid, point-of-service diagnostic tests and better physician education would provide critical situational awareness during public health crises; but thus far these matters have not been examined from a strategic perspective.

NBIS [National Biosurveillance Integration System, launched in 2004] may be intended to address this issue—at least in part—but it is difficult to find clear statements of what NBIS will accomplish, what data will be collected from where, how it will be analyzed, who will use the output, how it will work, or how much it will cost. The main flaw in NBIS as it is now described is the apparent assumption that there are lots of data sources available to be collated and analyzed. This is not the case, and a careful appraisal of what fundamental sources and types of data are needed and available is essential.

Moreover, recent experience across the federal government has shown that large, ambitious electronic information systems are difficult to build and most such programs fail. GAO [Government Accountability Office] has documented many reasons for these failures, including unclear goals, rapid turnover among and inadequately skilled project managers, failure to consult appropriately with stakeholders, inadequate funding, etc. Both the DHS's planned NBIS and CDC's [Centers for Disease Control and Prevention] BioSense programs are likely victims of such ills. Moreover, it is not at all evident that these ambitious electronic information systems will serve their intended purpose.

Specifically, I would suggest that national investments in rapid diagnostic tests and in electronic health records and digital links between hospitals and public health agencies will yield more benefits—for both routine and emergency use—than additional investments in environmental sensors or syndromic surveillance technologies. We should not have to decide between electronic health data or environmental sensors; rather there must be a coherent, long-term strategy for biosurveillance.

Assessing BioWatch

The governing concept of BioWatch, a collection of environmental sensors located in cities and critical locales across the U.S. and designed to detect specific airborne bioweapons agents, is that early detection of bioweapons pathogens in the air will enable an earlier "response" and thus save lives. DHS first deployed BioWatch in some cities just before U.S. troops entered Iraq in 2003, and has expanded the number of sensors and improved aspects of the technology and its management since then.

BioWatch is intended to supply "early warning" of an aerosolized bioattack. While early warning is desirable, there are a number of practical, operational, and strategic questions that deserve examination before additional investments are committed to the BioWatch program. It is not clear thus far, based on detection of natural organisms in the environment that were previously not known to be there, that BioWatch information alone is "actionable." That is, in several incidents of BioWatch detectors accurately signaling the presence of a pathogen, public health officials were reluctant to take decisive action—to act as though an attack were underway—without confirmatory clinical data. This raises questions about whether BioWatch truly shortens "response time."

Other important questions about BioWatch include the following:

- Will the turn-around time for BioWatch samples—i.e., the time required to collect the samples from the sensors, transport them to labs and analyze the filters— shorten the time needed to detect an attack large enough to be picked up by the sensors, or will astute clinicians recognize the attack just as quickly? Would cheap, rapid, point-of-service clinical diagnostic tests be a more cost-effective investment than the next generation of BioWatch?

- Does it make sense to invest limited biodefense funds in more advanced BioWatch technology even as we cut funds for public health personnel needed to analyze BioWatch data, as we are now doing? Many public health professionals at the March 15 White House meeting noted that assessment of BioWatch data requires limited public health resources that might be otherwise employed to greater effect.

- State and local public health officials—the "users" of these technologies who are the ones who must decide to act on BioWatch data—have repeatedly complained, at the March meeting and in Congressional hearings and roundtables, about lack of coordination and poor information flows. What is DHS doing to address these local concerns?

- Environmental sensor technologies are now being marketed to individual companies for installation in privately owned buildings. Will DHS develop commercial standards or regulations to ensure that such systems are reliable and maintained properly? Should public health agencies be required to assess every warning signal ("hit") registered by privately owned sensors? Should public health agencies be reimbursed for such assess ments?

- Would we improve detection more cost-effectively by focusing on raising clinicians' awareness of bioweapons-related diseases or by investments in point-of-care diagnostic tests, which not only could detect bioweapons agents but would help sort out attack victims once an attack occurs?

- Would digital connections between hospitals and public health agencies be more cost-effective and more widely useful than environmental sensors in detecting natural disease outbreaks and bioattacks? Such connections, which are now rare, would certainly be valuable in ascertaining situational awareness once an epidemic is underway.

- What are the long-term plans for BioWatch deployments? Thinking enemies are likely to learn which jurisdictions are covered by BioWatch and which areas of the country are less thoroughly monitored. The JAS-ONS [an independent scientific advisory group] calculated that sensor coverage of the entire country would cost $40 per person per year—$12 billion/year for all 300 million Americans. Is BioWatch expansion a smart use of limited biodefense resources? What are the operational advantages of deploying a third-generation technology as DHS proposes?

These are complicated questions. I want to acknowledge that DHS personnel have worked extremely hard to deploy BioWatch and to improve its technical performance and to coordinate response scenarios with local public health officials and first responders. However, I remain skeptical about the overall value of the program. . . .

The United States—for now—has the world's best scientific research base and the most powerful technological prowess, but our technical imagination has to be matched by strategic thinking and wise choices. We have made some progress in the past six years, but our activities to date do not reflect a commitment to a national security priority. It is time to think anew about the biothreat and what we should do about it.

| "Although much work remains . . . state and community preparedness levels overall have improved."

America Is Better Prepared for Bioterrorism Attacks

Aaron Katz, Andrea B. Staiti, and Kelly L. McKenzie

In the following viewpoint, Aaron Katz, Andrea B. Staiti, and Kelly L. McKenzie claim that since the 2001 terrorist attacks against the United States, federal, state, and local emergency response organizations have improved their overall preparedness for a bioterrorism attack. As the authors note, most authorities have used their federal and state funding wisely to purchase monitoring and communications equipment and to improve collaboration between various agencies that would respond to health threats. According to Katz and his colleagues, local and state organizations are continually testing their response staffs with live trials and have broadened their scope to bring bioterrorism response under an umbrella of health threat emergency strategies. Aaron Katz is a lecturer in the Department of Global Health at the University of Washington in Seattle. He also serves as a senior consulting researcher at the Center for Studying Health Sys-

Aaron Katz, Andrea B. Staiti, and Kelly L. McKenzie, "Preparing for the Unknown, Responding to the Known: Communities and Public Health Preparedness," *Health Affairs*, vol. 25, 2006, pp. 946–957. Reprinted by permission.

tem Change (HSC) in Washington, D.C., where both Andrea B. Staiti and Kelly L. McKenzie serve as researchers.

As you read, consider the following questions:

1. Why have communities used federal and state bioterrorism funding to invest in other health-related technologies and systems, according to Katz, Staiti, and McKenzie?

2. As the authors describe it, what was the TOPOFF exercise?

3. How many of the twelve Community Tracking Study sites experienced funding reductions during fiscal years 2003–2005, according to Katz, Staiti, and McKenzie?

More than four years after the September 11 terrorist strikes and subsequent anthrax scares in 2001, bioterrorism preparedness remains a high priority for federal, state, and local governments. This priority is reflected primarily in federal funding made available through the Centers for Disease Control and Prevention's (CDC's) Public Health Preparedness and Response for Bioterrorism cooperative agreement program and the Health Resources and Services Administration's (HRSA's) National Bioterrorism Hospital Preparedness Program. Department of Homeland Security (DHS) programs, such as the Metropolitan Medical Response System and the Urban Area Security Initiative, also fund large metropolitan areas to improve emergency preparedness.

Using these funds, state and local governments have strengthened their ability to respond to public health emergencies, adding capacity that will be useful not only in large-scale events but also for everyday functions that protect communities' health. Federal funding has allowed jurisdictions to improve disease surveillance, communication, and laboratory capacity, although past reports suggest that improvements are not consistent across communities.[1] Local public health officials have developed closer working relationships with various partners around preparedness planning. Activities such as those focused on bioterrorism threats and distribution of pharmaceutical stockpiles brought public health officials together with emergency management, police, fire departments, and medical care providers in collaborations that once were rare.[2] However, these earlier reports noted several challenges, such as public health workforce shortages, barriers to regional coordination, incompatible communication systems, and lack of surge capacity.[3] Also, balancing their attention between bioterrorism preparedness and other public health priorities has proved difficult for public health agencies, especially given that states have cut some public health funding in recent years.[4]

Building on the Center for Studying Health System Change's (HSC's) findings in 2002–03, this report examines the progress communities have made two years later in their ability to respond to public health emergencies.

Study Data and Methods

Our findings are based on data collected during biennial site visits for the Community Tracking Study (CTS), a longitudinal study conducted by HSC. Site visits for Round Five of the CTS occurred between January and June 2005 and included interviews with more than 1,000 health system leaders from a wide range of organizations across twelve nationally representative markets.[5]

Public health was the focus of 155 telephone and in-person interviews across the twelve sites. In each community, we sought to interview three local public health agency executives, a community partner in public health (an organization that collaborates with the local health agency), executives at up to five hospitals, two community health center (CHC) executives, and a market-vantage respondent. We also inter-

Exhibit 1: Events In Twelve Communities That Tested Public Health Preparedness, 2003–2005

Site	Live-fire exercises	Public health emergencies
Boston	Democratic National Convention (2004); World Series (2004)	Hepatitis A outbreak (2004)
Cleveland	Flu vaccine shortage (2004–05); International Children's Games (2004)	Helicopter crash (2005); midwest blackout (2003)
Greenville		Train wreck with chlorine release (2004)
Indianapolis	Flu vaccine shortage (2004–05)	Hepatitis A scare (2004)
Lansing		Midwest blackout (2003); 200-car pileup in snowstorm (2005)
Little Rock	Flu vaccine shortage (2004–05)	Airline crash (100 people) (2003)
Miami		Hurricanes (2004)
Northern New Jersey		Airplane crash and large fire (2005)
Orange County	Flu vaccine shortage (2004–05)	Train wreck (2003); hospital power failure (2004)
Phoenix	Flu vaccine shortage (2004–05)	Three water treatment facilities shut down (2005)
Seattle	Flu vaccine shortage (2004–05)	Pertussis outbreak (2004–05)
Syracuse	Flu vaccine shortage (2004–05); Republican National Convention (2004)	Hospital bomb scare (2004); blackout (2003)

SOURCE: Information derived from Community Tracking Study (CTS) site-visit interviews conducted January–June 2005.

viewed representatives of state health departments as well as one federal public health agency and one national public health association.

The interviews included questions about changes in public health funding; effects of funding changes on bioterrorism preparedness and other public health priorities; changes in public health capacity; agencies' ability to balance competing priorities; and the usefulness of previously formed bioterrorism preparedness collaborations in the pursuit of other public health priorities.

Study Findings

New Public Health Priorities Emerge Bioterrorism preparedness remains a high priority in the CTS sites.[6] States and communities continue to dedicate generous resources to preparedness activities, and the ability to respond to a terrorist attack remains an overarching concern for health departments. Although much work remains to improve infrastructure and address remaining deficiencies, respondents indicated that state and community preparedness levels overall have improved since 2001. As a result, the emphasis on bioterrorism preparedness has evolved from expansion of capabilities to sustainability, allowing public health departments to direct more attention toward traditional public health activities such as childhood immunizations, infectious disease control, and chronic disease prevention.

Although bioterrorism preparedness remains a top priority, many state and local health officials indicated that during the past two years, health departments have focused more effort on other public health concerns. These priorities ranged from lead poisoning, smoking, maternal and child health, health disparities, dental care access, and cancer to preventing and responding to outbreaks of communicable diseases such as tuberculosis (TB), HIV/AIDS, and West Nile virus. As is often the case, emphasis on these items varied from community to community, based on factors such as the burden of specific diseases, political leadership and community activity around specific health issues, and the amount of funding available. For example, HIV/AIDS is a key issue in northern New Jersey, where the already-high prevalence rate of HIV continues to climb. Respondents reported that CDC and Ryan White funding allowed them to undertake new efforts to combat the disease. In Little Rock, respondents were most concerned about childhood obesity, a top priority of Gov. Mike Huckabee. Key stakeholders have embraced his obesity prevention initiatives, some of which provide funding for community programs.

Chronic disease prevention, however, emerged as a priority across states and communities. Nationally, this issue has received increased attention in recent years, with federal programs such as Steps to a Healthier US providing funding for selected communities (including Boston, Cleveland, and Seattle among CTS sites) to undertake prevention activities related to asthma, diabetes, and obesity.[7] In Indianapolis, the local health department is promoting healthy lifestyles through the fitness program Indy in Motion, and South Carolina has launched the Healthy South Carolina Initiative to improve family fitness. In Arkansas, enactment of the 2003 Child Health Initiative and Governor Huckabee's highly publicized weight loss in 2004 led to a number of obesity-related initiatives, including measuring the body mass index of all elementary school children.

Infrastructure Improvements. Generally, respondents felt that the federal government's "all-hazards approach" has facilitated investments that benefit the public health system as a whole. Most communities reported using bioterrorism funding to create multiple-use systems that can respond to a range of events including terrorism. By investing in such areas as communications, epidemiology, and lab capacity, health departments have strengthened core functions that contribute to the success of various public health activities.

State and local health departments reported improved communication among providers, health departments, and other emergency response agencies as a result of bioterrorism funding. They have invested in new communication tools, such as radio systems, online alert networks, and new computer equipment, which are essential for effective responses to terrorist events or other emergencies. For example, the Ohio Department of Health now has a dedicated cable line to instantly communicate with local health departments about health threats as they arise, vastly improving response time and coordination. A Michigan county outfitted its communicable disease unit with computers and software programs and set up a county communications center, to enable quicker response times.

Health departments have also used bioterrorism preparedness funding to hire risk communicators, preparedness coordinators, and epidemiologists to address emerging needs related to bioterrorism. Because their expertise can be applied to other functions, some health departments report that the new staff have helped offset staff cuts in other public health programs resulting from state and local budget shortfalls.

Increased staffing levels have also enhanced health departments' lab capabilities. Most states with CTS sites have upgraded their public health laboratories to handle anthrax samples and other hazardous agents in the aftermath of 9/11, requiring additional staff. Similarly, hiring epidemiologists and statisticians (and investing in computer equipment) has led to improved disease surveillance. The Florida Department of Health has used preparedness funds to integrate its surveillance systems and collect data in a central database, allowing for more rapid and streamlined health threat analyses. Although focused initially on bioterrorism preparedness, this new capability will support efforts to address many types of disease outbreaks. Boston and Seattle have implemented "syndromic surveillance" systems that collect information in real time from hospitals, pharmacies, and other sources so that public health officials can detect spikes or clusters of symptoms that might indicate a disease outbreak.

Local health departments also reported that the overall preparation process for bioterrorism disasters has improved their ability to evaluate and respond to various public health threats. Respondents feel better prepared for any emergency. One of the main benefits of the bioterrorism planning process has been the opportunity to collaborate with other actors in the emergency response system.

Ongoing Collaborations. As reported two years ago, the 2001 terrorist attacks highlighted the need for much closer communication and coordination across sectors.[8] Previously, many public health agencies had limited contact with law enforcement and other emergency response personnel. Agencies have had to work through differences in their organizational cultures and approaches to managing emergencies to work together and understand each other's roles. These efforts have led to ongoing collaborations among local public health agencies, law enforcement, fire departments, emergency medical services (EMS), and hospitals and to increased interaction between federal, state, and local agencies. The 2005 site visits revealed that these collaborations have continued and, in most communities, have grown stronger. Some public health agencies are now reaching out to additional partners, such as schools, private businesses, and other nongovernmental agencies.

Respondents indicated that the relationships formed for bioterrorism preparedness are useful for responding to naturally occurring emergencies. For example, Cleveland respondents described the partnerships between agencies and organizations as critical during the 2003 blackout. Miami respondents said that bioterrorism trainings and disaster preparedness drills fostered a high level of cooperation among various players in the emergency response system that, in turn, resulted in smoother responses to a series of hurricanes in 2004.

Collaborations formed around preparedness efforts also have been useful in addressing infectious disease outbreaks and distributing flu vaccines. For example, existing collaborations aided responses to a pertussis outbreak in Seattle in 2004–05 and a hepatitis A outbreak in Boston in 2004. Also, many communities activated their bioterrorism vaccine dissemination plans to distribute flu vaccine in 2005, using relationships among public health agencies, the medical community, and organizations such as the Red Cross. Such relationships largely have not been helpful for other public health priorities, however, such as chronic disease prevention and anti-obesity efforts, which typically do not include emergency response personnel.

Testing Under Fire. Communities have had numerous opportunities to test the investments they have made in public health preparedness and examine the extent to which their capacities have improved. We have organized these opportunities into three categories: planned preparedness exercises, "live-fire" tests, and public health emergencies; examples of the latter two are shown in Exhibit 1.

Planned preparedness exercises. These exercises include community-specific or nationally coordinated drills designed to test local response capacity. Community drills—which could be tabletop exercises or simulated events in the field—are designed to test such capabilities as emergency communication systems, vaccine distribution, and command-and-control structures. For example, Miami conducted a tabletop exercise involving a maritime terrorist threat that involved port authorities, cruise lines, physicians, and others. A bioterrorism exercise in New Jersey tested collaboration among the local police, fire departments, and the University Hospital's EMS system.

Exhibit 2: Changes in Public Health Preparedness Funding Nationally and in Twelve States, 2003–2005

Public health preparedness and hospital preparedness funding (thousands of dollars)

Site	FY 2003			FY 2005			% change, 2003–2005
	CDC	HRSA	Total to jurisdiction	CDC	HRSA	Total to jurisdiction	
AZ	15,755	9,030	24,785	17,067	8,964	26,031	5.03
AR	10,461	5,078	15,539	9,302	4,634	13,936	-10.31
CA	55,590	38,774	94,363	61,339	39,203	100,543	6.55
FL	38,182	25,776	63,958	39,221	26,311	65,532	2.46
IN	17,416	10,271	27,687	16,461	9,897	26,358	-4.80
MA	17,973	10,686	28,659	17,872	10,257	28,129	-1.85
MI	25,279	16,141	41,420	27,106	10,257	37,363	-9.80
NJ	22,249	13,879	36,127	21,953	13,601	35,555	-1.59
NY	27,794	18,020	45,814	28,293	17,748	46,041	0.50
OH	28,082	18,235	46,317	27,902	17,844	45,746	-1.23
SC	13,232	7,147	20,379	12,109	6,790	18,899	-7.26
WA	17,146	10,069	27,215	17,351	9,799	27,150	-0.24
US	870,000	498,000	1,368,000	862,770	470,755	1,333,532	-2.52

SOURCES: U.S. Department of Health and Human Services, "HHS Announces $1.3 Billion in Funding to States for Bioterrorism Preparedness," Press Release, 13 May 2005, http://hhs.gov/news/press/2005pres/20050513.html (accessed 19 April 2006); and DHHS, "HHS Announces Bioterrorism Aid for States, Including Special Opportunity for Advance Funding," Press Release, 20 March 2003, http://www.hhs.gov/news/press/2003pres/20030320.html (accessed 19 April 2006).

NOTES: CDC is Centers for Disease Control and Prevention. HRSA is Health Resources and Services Administration.

The DHS has coordinated multisite tests called Top Officials, or TOPOFF, exercises involving federal, state, and local agencies. These congressionally mandated exercises, which focus on threats from weapons of mass destruction, involve a series of seminars and planning events that led up to a full-scale terrorist attack simulation. Since 2000, three TOPOFF exercises have been conducted, two involving CTS communities: Seattle and Chicago in TOPOFF 2 and New Jersey and Connecticut in TOPOFF 3.

"Live-fire" tests. Live-fire tests are large-scale planned events in a community—such as sporting events or conventions—that offer public health agencies and their partners opportunities to test their preparedness capacities in real-life situations. For example, Cleveland hosted the International Children's Games in 2004, which allowed the city to activate its emergency operations center. Boston did the same for the Democratic National Convention and World Series that same year, especially testing its partnerships with state and federal agencies.

Public health emergencies. Actual public health emergencies often revealed most clearly the strengths and weaknesses of local public health preparedness efforts. Nearly all twelve CTS sites reported that the flu vaccine episode in 2004–05 tested their ability to respond quickly to a sudden surge in demand, such as might occur in a smallpox terrorist attack. In fall 2004, public health officials strongly urged vulnerable people to get vaccinated. A manufacturing problem with one of two major suppliers caused a severe shortage and large pent-up demand. When vaccine shortages eased in early 2005 and demand spiked, many locales activated their bioterrorism vaccine dissemination plans, creating temporary clinics or moving vaccine quickly to hospitals. Observers in most sites reported that these efforts were successful and validated many of their preparedness efforts.

More urgent emergencies also challenged response capacities. In Boston, officials faced two consecutive hepatitis A outbreaks, one that required inoculation of 2,500 people in two days and the second involving 900 people. These outbreaks tested the city's surge capacity, incident command structure, stockpile planning, volunteer training procedures, and risk communication plans. It also tested coordination among EMS, schools (for buses), the transportation department, and the emergency call center. Lansing, Syracuse, and Cleveland responded to multiple threats during the Midwest power grid failure in 2003 by mobilizing their respective emergency operation centers. The lack of electricity highlighted gaps in backup power for water systems and sewage treatment, as well as for telephone systems. In response, Lansing purchased "old simple operating phones" that don't require electricity. Three water treatment facilities in Phoenix shut down in early 2005, causing a "boil water" order that revealed inadequate preparation for public information and risk communication. Large-scale vehicular accidents also tested emergency response, surge capacity, and interagency communications and coordination in Greenville, Lansing, and Little Rock.

Remaining Challenges. Observers generally reported that planned exercises, live-fire tests, and public health emergencies showed improvements in public health capacity as a result of new infrastructure and collaborative relationships. They also reported that challenges remain, particularly in sustainable funding, provider capacity, public health workforce, competing priorities, and jurisdictional confusion.

Funding. In most communities, the most important funding sources for public health preparedness are the CDC and HRSA programs. Through these programs, Congress has made the first major investment in basic capacity building for public health agencies in recent memory. New funds, however, along with the publicity around terrorist threats and their prevention, have "raised expectations about preparedness and our ability to respond by the programs and initiatives we've put in place," explained one local health official. Public health leaders in a number of CTS sites voiced concern about their ability to meet these expectations over time, given questions about the sustainability of federal funding.

Total public health and hospital preparedness funding from the CDC and HRSA dropped 3 percent from FY 2003 to FY 2005, from $1.37 billion to $1.33 billion.[9] Eight of the twelve CTS sites experienced funding reductions during this period (Exhibit 2). The overall drop in federal funding has been exacerbated in some communities by the redirection in 2004 of some funds from states (which pass funds through to communities) to cities that are projected to be at highest risk of attack. The Cities Readiness Initiative (CRI) was blamed by some local health officials for the reductions in their pre-paredness grants.[10] For example, respondents in Lansing at-tributed its drop in funding to Detroit's new CRI grant.

Federal cuts have been magnified in some communities by concurrent cuts in state support for public health, despite fed-eral nonsupplantation provisions. Respondents noted that state public health funding in Arkansas had dropped every year for the past twenty years, and Indiana's public health budget dropped 17 percent from 2004 to 2005. In some com-munities, the combination of state and federal cuts has left lo-cal governments holding the bag. As a respondent in Lansing said, "If federal support slows or goes away, this will dump these obligations on local officials. Because of increased expec-tations, it will be hard for local officials not to continue such efforts, but to do so will mean hurting some other services."

Provider capacity. Hospitals, and to a lesser extent other health care providers, have improved their ability to respond to public health threats, but observers are not confident of their ability to handle large-scale emergencies. Most hospitals reported being involved in meetings with public health and emergency management officials and, for the most part, indicated that they are more prepared than they were two years ago, through acquisition of new equipment such as decontamination showers and isolation units. Some hospitals reported, however, that funding wasn't sufficient to make adequate investments, particularly for improving information systems and training staff. For example, a hospital in Miami noted gaps in its technological capabilities and computer equipment that would allow it to track emergent events. Several hospitals reported that finding time and money to train staff was an ongoing concern, particularly given staff turnover.

In almost all communities, hospitals expressed concerns about having the standby capacity to handle a sudden spike of patients in a terrorist attack, natural disaster, or epidemic. Large hospitals, especially those that anchor community safety nets, often operate at or near capacity, so their ability to serve a large influx of critical patients is limited. As one hospital chief executive officer (CEO) remarked, "The notion of having surge capacity in the community to deal with a large-scale disaster is really pie in the sky." Hospital officials also face a daunting array of possible threats, from chemical to nuclear to biological, which are challenging even to the best of planners. The predicament was voiced by one emergency department (ED) director, who wondered, "How much do you really prepare for the unknown? How many victims do you plan for? No one can really tell us."

CHCs may be well situated in some communities to be a first line of response to public health emergencies. Two years ago, CHCs in the twelve CTS communities were largely uninvolved in bioterrorism preparedness efforts. The 2005 site visits revealed that CHCs' preparedness has improved. Some states are allocating HRSA funds to CHCs, in addition to hospitals, which have in turn attended training meetings, purchased equipment, and evaluated their policies and plans. For example, a CHC in northern New Jersey has received funding in increments of about $5,000 for training or equipment. In at least a few communities, CHC directors expressed concerns about not having the capacity to handle large-scale events. In the words of one director, "We could handle a few more earaches. . . . We are short-term focused and have lots of day-to-day challenges we have to deal with." Rather than being able to serve a large influx of patients, some respondents see a role for CHCs in providing risk communication with the public, particularly in communities with diverse languages and cultures.

Staffing. Public health agency staffing continues to be a challenge for states and communities. In 2004 the Association of State and Territorial Health Officials (ASTHO) reported that, on average, 24 percent of the public health workforce is eligible for retirement, and that figure is as high as 45 percent for some state public health agencies.[11] Staffing problems stem in part from a short supply of public health workers and an inability to offer competitive salaries. Some respondents reported that budget constraints have caused hiring restrictions at the state and local levels. For example, public health staffing has eroded in California in recent years, and observers said that the state health department is now operating at roughly 60–70 percent of its capacity of ten years ago. In fact, bioterrorism staff are the agency's only new hires, while hiring in other areas has been frozen or cut back. State officials from Michigan and Indiana also reported being unable to employ sufficient public health staff. Respondents from Orange County especially noted trouble recruiting public health nurses.

Competing priorities. Across the twelve communities, local public health agencies indicated that balancing competing priorities continues to be very difficult. Although preparedness funding has clearly helped bolster public health infrastructure, some community respondents question the amount of money devoted to bioterrorism preparedness planning versus more day-to-day public health concerns, such as immunizations, sexually transmitted diseases (STDs), and TB prevention. For example, an ED manager in Seattle questioned having to spend time preparing for an unlikely terrorist attack when "real-life" challenges must be faced every day, such as flu epidemics among the homeless population. One public health official described a disproportionate amount of money being allocated to the "virtual disease" of bioterrorism rather than real disease such as TB.

Jurisdictional confusion. Potential conflicts and gaps between the responsibilities of federal, state, and local officials have long been recognized as an impediment to public health preparedness.[12] Despite collaborations and improved communication among stakeholders, a few observers noted remaining jurisdictional issues. For example, in Miami during Hurricane Ivan in 2004, emergency responders were confused over who was in charge of a central shelter facility. Interviewees suggested that the reorganization of federal agencies for homeland security left uncertainty over the roles of the DHS, the Federal Emergency Management Agency (FEMA), and the U.S. Department of Health and Human Services (HHS); and the state health department had a difficult time figuring out which agency to contact for which issue. Respondents in Boston expressed similar frustrations, because each major federal agency involved in preparedness efforts (CDC, DHS, and HRSA) has its own regional structure whose geographic boundaries match neither those of other federal agencies nor those of local emergency response agencies. These noncontiguous jurisdictions reportedly caused duplicative efforts in some cases and conflicts in others. As one respondent remarked, "They used to say that all emergencies are local; now all emergencies are federal."

Ongoing Improvements

Preparedness is a process, not a destination. The U.S. Government Accountability Office (GAO) found in 2004 that "no state is fully prepared to respond to a major public health threat."[13] Our visits in 2005 revealed ongoing challenges to and gaps in communities' ability to respond to large-scale disasters. Indeed, both public health and hospital officials raised questions about whether communities could ever be prepared for the full range of potential disasters. "There are so many unknowns," said one observer in Little Rock. "It would be one thing if you only had to worry about one situation, but when you look at the scope of things that could happen, I think there will always be gaps."

Nonetheless, we found that the capabilities of local public health and emergency response agencies are much improved from two years ago. Overwhelmingly, respondents attributed this progress to the large influx of federal funding whose benefits have accrued to basic public health functions. With few exceptions, state and local health officials praised CDC funding, because they were able to beef up these essential capacities that had eroded through long years of funding neglect. In the eyes of these leaders, funding that is ongoing and flexible is key.

The ongoing nature of the funding has been critical, as most improvements revealed in our site visits were not one-time investments but rather required years of effort. The intersectoral collaborations among public health, fire, police, and emergency management agencies are a prime example. These groups have different cultures and approaches to emergency response and public communication. Overcoming these differences requires the development of working, trusting relationships, where often none existed, and maintaining such relationships requires ongoing nurturing through regular meetings and planning exercises. Likewise, building the capacity of staff to take on multiple responsibilities during disasters requires a continuous series of training sessions as new techniques and lessons are learned and as trained staffers leave and new ones are hired.

Agencies' ability to use the CDC funds to strengthen core public health functions was a departure from years of categorical funding, which often undermines a community's ability to prepare for a wide range of threats. Public health agencies have considerable experience with funds restricted to HIV/AIDS, maternal and child health, TB, and the like. Respondents in 2003 voiced concern that bioterrorism preparedness would be just one more in the long line of vertical programs; starting in 2003, federal authorities pushed efforts to prepare for a smallpox bioterrorism event, which some local and state officials feared would divert attention and resources from other, more plausible, public health threats.[14] Our interviews in 2005 found that nothing came of fears that bioterrorism preparedness would become another categorical program.

Although public health and its emergency-response partners reported much progress in their potential to respond to public health threats, the picture of the health care system is less sanguine. Funding from HRSA's National Bioterrorism Hospital Preparedness Program had to be dispersed to thousands of hospitals, meaning that few hospitals received more than a few thousand dollars—enough only to purchase equipment such as isolation suits and provide one-time training to staff. Hospitals' big challenges, however, involve having sufficient space and staff to treat large numbers of patients who need immediate attention after a biological, chemical, or nuclear terrorist attack. The hospital CEOs and ED directors we interviewed, as well as respondents from CHCs and medical practices, were nearly unanimous in their view that given capacity limitations, they could not accommodate the large surges in demand envisioned by worst-case scenarios.

Lessons from Recent Disasters

When the tsunami hit Southern Asia on 26 December 2004, we learned quickly of the absence of early-warning surveillance systems, emergency communication networks, and response planning in the Indian Ocean region. But when Hurricane Katrina wreaked havoc on the U.S. Gulf Coast on 29 August 2005, we realized that our own level of emergency preparedness and response was inadequate, even after four years of intense planning activities and the investment of billions of dollars. If we could pick our disasters, we might be able to prepare for them, but disasters of the scope of the tsunami and Katrina stretch the outer bounds of what communities might ever be prepared for. Yet even if we can't be "fully" prepared, we can be better prepared. Our study found that sizable increases in funding for basic public health infrastructure can lead to improved community preparedness and hinted that retrenchment from this investment could erode newfound capacity. The current threat of pandemic avian flu raises the ante for policymakers to learn from this experience.

Notes

1. M. McHugh, A.B. Staiti, and L.E. Felland, "How Prepared Are Americans for Public Health Emergencies? Twelve Communities Weigh In," *Health Affairs* 23, no. 3 (2004): 201–209; and U.S. Government Accountability Office, *Infectious Disease Outbreaks: Bioterrorism Preparedness Efforts Have Improved Public Health Response Capacity, but Gaps Remain*, Pub. no. GAO-03-654T (Washington: GAO, 2003).

2. A.B. Staiti, A. Katz, and J.F. Hoadley, "Has Bioterrorism Preparedness Improved Public Health?" Issue Brief no. 65 (Washington: Center for Studying Health System Change, 2003).

3. GAO, *Public Health Preparedness: Response Capacity Improving, but Much Remains to Be Accomplished*, Pub. no. GAO-04-458T (Washington: GAO, 2004).

4. Staiti et al., "Has Bioterrorism Preparedness Improved Public Health?"

5. The twelve communities were Boston; Cleveland; Green-ville, South Carolina; Indianapolis; Lansing; Little Rock; Miami; northern New Jersey; Orange County, California; Phoenix; Seattle; and Syracuse. They were randomly selected from among large metropolitan areas with populations of more than 200,000.

6. The terms "bioterrorism preparedness" and "public health preparedness" are often used interchangeably in public health discussions, reflecting inherent ambiguity in the CDC and HRSA programs. Although the names of both programs include the term "bioterrorism," guidance provided to state and local health officials discusses an "all hazards" approach; that is, funding is to be used for planning and capacity building that addresses a broad array of public health threats in addition to bioterrorism. In this paper we use "bioterrorism preparedness" to refer to preparedness efforts targeted specifically to terrorist threats and "public health preparedness" for efforts that target both natural and human-created public health threats. "Emergency preparedness" refers to the capacity to respond to emergencies of all types, including public health emergencies.

7. CDC, "Steps to a Healthier US: Cooperative Agreement Program, Funding Communities to Prevent Obesity, Diabetes, and Asthma, FY 2004," http://www.healthierus.gov/steps/grantees/2004/StepsCoopAgrmn.pdf (accessed 18 April 2006).

8. Staiti et al., "Has Bioterrorism Improved Public Health?"

9. U.S. Department of Health and Human Services, "HHS Announces $1.3 Billion in Funding to States for Bioterrorism Preparedness," 13 May 2005, http://www.hhs.gov/news/press/2005pres/20050513.html (accessed 18 April 2006); and DHHS, "HHS Announces Bioterrorism Aid for States, Including Special Opportunity for Advance Funding," 20 March 2003, http://www.hhs.gov/news/press/2003pres/20030320.html (accessed 18 April 2006).

10. Begun in FY 2004, the Cities Readiness Initiative (CRI) is a pilot program through which the CDC redirects some public health preparedness funds from states and local health departments to twenty cities (including Boston, Cleveland, Miami, Phoenix, and Seattle among CTS sites) and the District of Columbia. The CRI aims to improve these cities' ability to dispense medicine and medical supplies from the Strategic National Stockpile in case of a large-scale bioterrorism attack or nuclear accident.

11. Association of State and Territorial Health Officials, "State Public Health Employee Worker Shortage Report," 2004, http://www.astho.org/pubs/Workforce-Survey-Report-2.pdf (accessed 17 May 2006).

12. ASTHO, *Preparedness Planning for State Health Officials: Nature's Terrorist Attack—Pandemic Influenza*, November 2002, http://www.astho.org/pubs/Pandemic%20Influenza .pdf (accessed 17 May 2006).

13. GAO, *Public Health Preparedness*.

14. Staiti et al., "Has Bioterrorism Preparedness Improved Public Health?"

> "[During the H1N1 pandemic,] a host
> of nations revealed themselves as deter-
> minedly and self-destructively commit-
> ted to their individual political inter-
> ests."

Nations Have Not Shown Willingness to Overcome Self-Interest in Fighting Pandemics

John Barry

In the viewpoint that follows, John Barry claims that the world did not learn the right lessons from the outbreak of H1N1 swine flu in 2009. Barry maintains that instead of working coopera- tively to combat the flu, many nations—the United States in- cluded—acted in their own self-interest, hoarding vaccines, claiming the flu was a "foreign" disease, and lying to their own people to contain hysteria. Barry asserts that such acts destroy trust between nations and erode the credibility of governments. In his opinion, if nations cannot learn to respond appropriately to global health crises, the next flu epidemic could have far greater and deadlier consequences than the H1N1 scare. John

John Barry, "The Next Pandemic," *World Policy Journal*, vol. 27, Summer 2010, pp. 10–12. Reprinted by permission of MIT Press.

Barry is a scholar at the Tulane/Xavier Center for Bioenvironmental Research in Louisiana and the author of The Great Influenza: The Story of the Deadliest Pandemic in History.

As you read, consider the following questions:

1. According to Barry, what policies will likely improve in response to the H1N1 pandemic?

2. As Barry reports, what two entities became the scapegoats for critics who believe the world overreacted to the H1N1 swine flu outbreak?

3. As the author states, why did Indonesia's health minister tell the citizens of his country that they would not be threatened by H1N1?

It is the nature of the influenza virus to cause pandemics. There have been at least 11 in the last 300 years, and there will certainly be another one, and one after that, and another after that. And it is impossible to predict whether a pandemic will be mild or lethal.

In 1997 in Hong Kong, the H5N1 virus jumped directly from chickens to 18 people, killing six. Public health officials slaughtered hundreds of thousands of ducks, chickens and other fowl to prevent further spread, and the virus seemed contained. It wasn't. In 2004, H5N1 returned with a vengeance. Since then, it has killed hundreds of millions of birds, while several hundred million more have been culled in prevention efforts. And it has infected more than 500 human beings, killing 60 percent of those infected. The virus's high mortality rate and memories of the 1918 influenza—the best estimates of that death toll range from 35 to 100 million people—got the world's attention. Every developed nation prepared for a pandemic, as did local and regional governments and the private sector. They all based their preparations on a 1918-like scenario, but it did not come. It still could.

Swine Flu Disoriented Nations

In March 2009, another influenza pandemic caused by a different virus did arrive, and it was nothing like the lethal one we expected. This particular H1N1 virus generated a pandemic with the lowest case mortality rate of any known outbreak in history. Nothing the world did accounted for the low death toll; it was simply luck that this pandemic virus had low lethality. The World Health Organization [WHO] counts fewer than 20,000 dead worldwide, but that's only laboratory-confirmed cases. It is impossible to know whether actual mortality was 10 or even 100 times that number.

But even the highest reasonable estimate of those killed by this latest pandemic so far—we could still see more waves of infection—still falls far below the anticipated scenario. The world assumed that preparing for a severe pandemic would allow it to adjust easily to a mild one. It was mistaken. This lesser pandemic threw the world off-balance, and very few nations have, with respect to influenza, regained their footing.

Not Learning the Right Lessons

The 2009 pandemic put the world under pressure and revealed flaws in both health systems and, more significantly, in international relations. The lessons we might learn from this past event could be of value in our ongoing war against the flu virus. But we're still getting too many things wrong.

Virologists, epidemiologists, public health officials, even ethicists and logisticians are analyzing data from the pandemic. Based on their results, health organizations will likely adopt modest management changes. The WHO previously defined an influenza pandemic as basically any occurrence in which a new influenza virus enters the human population and passes easily between humans; it may refine that definition by adding a virulence factor, similar to the Saffir-Simpson scale for hurricanes (category 1 to category 5). Vaccine delivery systems will improve. Local hospitals will upgrade their triage practices. And some fundamental changes which were already underway—such as shifting vaccine production away from chicken eggs, a technology used for more than half a century, to new production technologies—will accelerate.

These are good starting points. But on larger policy and scientific questions any efforts to draw conclusions could mislead. All other pandemics we know about in any detail—in 1918, 1957 and 1968—sickened 25 percent of the population or more in every country for which data exists. The 2009 data suggests attack rates approached that benchmark figure in children only, while adults were generally attacked at only a quarter to a half that rate, not because of any public health measures taken but most likely because adults had already been exposed to a similar virus and had some immunity. This distinctly unusual pattern makes it difficult to draw conclusions on the effectiveness of, for example, such non-pharmaceutical interventions as screening airport arrivals or shutting down schools. Yet some epidemiologists are insisting on doing just that. Policy for the next pandemic is being set, and it is based on the analysis of *sui generis* [unique] data.

Irrationally Blaming the WHO

The world needs to learn the right political lessons, too, and so far it has shown no sign of doing so. Instead, a scapegoat is being groomed. The WHO has come under intense attack for declaring a pandemic at all, and critics have even charged the pharmaceutical industry with influencing the decision. This is nonsense. The spring of 1918 saw a mild initial flu much like 2009—so mild, in fact, that the British Grand Fleet patrolling Europe's coast had 10,313 sailors sick enough to miss duty during war, but only four died. Yet several months later, Armageddon arrived. Aware of that history, the WHO was all but compelled to act as it did. If the current criticism of the WHO makes it more cautious in the future, the world will become a more dangerous place.

The real overreaction came not from the WHO but from the nations that ignored the accurate epidemiological and clinical information the WHO regularly released. These countries refused to adjust their response and implemented extreme measures, either out of irrational fears or for domestic political reasons.

Punishing Mexico

The world needs transparency about disease. Mexico, where H1N1 first appeared in humans, told the truth, and for this it was roundly punished. Since there was no possibility of containing the virus, WHO and FAO [Food and Agriculture Organization] explicitly recommended against trade or travel restrictions. Yet at least 25 countries limited trade with or travel to Mexico. France demanded that the EU [European Union] suspend all flights there, and although that did not happen, the EU and the U.S. government recommended canceling non-essential travel to Mexico—although the U.S. soon had more cases of H1N1. The World Bank estimated that this mild pandemic cost the Mexican economy 0.7 percent of GDP [gross domestic product]. Such political reaction makes the world less safe, since it makes countries less likely to tell the truth for fear of the repercussions.

Even more disturbing, a host of nations revealed themselves as determinedly and self-destructively committed to their individual political interests. It should surprise no one that the United States promised last September [2009] to give some vaccine to countries without any, then retracted the promise when production lagged, saying it first had to protect its own vulnerable population. But breaking a commitment sets a dangerous precedent—the United States imports almost 70 percent of its vaccine. In a severe pandemic, political leaders of an exporting country could refuse to allow their manufacturers to ship supplies to the United States until its own population is protected, and cite this U.S. precedent.

National Irrationality

At least hoarding vaccine to protect your domestic population is rational. The pandemic also demonstrated the irrationality of nations. Egypt exploited the outbreak to slaughter all pigs, a popular act since Muslims don't eat pork. Several countries either lied or all but totally misunderstood the threat. Indonesia's health minister told his citizens they had no need to worry about H1N1 because they lived in a tropical climate. Chinese Health Minister Chen Zhu initially declared, "We are confident and capable of preventing and containing an H1N1 influenza epidemic." Yet this is, literally, impossible. In late September, with H1N1 already throughout China, he said his country would focus its vaccine effort on areas with the greatest interaction with foreigners since it remained "a foreign disease."

Such actions neither encourage nor reflect transparency, and destroy trust between nations. They are counterproductive domestically, undermining a government's credibility. Above all, they too make the world a more dangerous place.

In 2009 the world in effect took a test. At the scientific and technocratic levels, it did reasonably well. But at the level where politicians operate, too many countries failed, and failed miserably. That does not portend well for the future.

The H5N1 virus continues to infect and kill. It's still a threat as a pandemic, while HIV and SARS [severe acute respiratory syndrome] demonstrate that new infectious diseases can emerge at any time. Meanwhile, a sense of complacency seems to be settling over the world. Because H5N1 has not become pandemic and H1N1 turned out to be mild, the idea that influenza is no longer a threat has become pervasive. Everything that happened in 2009 suggests that, if a severe outbreak comes again, failure to improve on our response will threaten chaos and magnify the terror, the economic impact and the death toll. And it will come again.

Periodical and Internet Sources Bibliography

The following articles have been selected to supplement the diverse views presented in this chapter.

Z. Ahmad	"The Very Real Threat of Bioterrorism: Are We Prepared?" *Internet Journal of Rescue & Disaster Medicine*, 2009. www.ispub.com/journal/ the_internet_journal_of_rescue_and_disaster _medicine.html.
Heike Baumüller and David L. Heymann	"Hooves and Humans," *World Today*, March 2010.
Carren Bersch	"Predicting Disaster," *MLO: Medical Laboratory Observer*, January 2010.
Debora MacKenzie	"The End for Flu Viruses: One Vaccine to Thwart Them All," *New Scientist*, August 22, 2009.
Arnold S. Monto	"The Risk of Seasonal and Pandemic Influenza: Prospects for Control," *Clinical Infectious Diseases*, January 1, 2009.
Klaus Stöhr	"Vaccinate Before the Next Pandemic?" *Nature*, May 13, 2010.
Liz Szabo	"Ill-Equipped for a Pandemic," *USA Today*, May 14, 2009.
Nathan Wolfe	"Preventing the Next Pandemic," *Scientific American*, April 2009.
Peter F. Wright	"Vaccine Preparedness—Are We Ready for the Next Influenza Pandemic?" *New England Journal of Medicine*, June 12, 2008.

For Further Discussion

Chapter 1

1. Colin Schultz claims the news media often misrepresent the dangers of infectious diseases by engaging in dramatic hyperbole, by misusing facts and figures, and by failing to understand the science behind the diseases. Do you believe Schultz's argument? Can you find examples in the media of misleading, overblown, or inaccurate statements relating to emergent diseases? Explain why the coverage you find might be a public disservice.

2. Clare Wilson reports that some medical authorities believe the AIDS pandemic can be eliminated by testing and treating at-risk populations to keep the disease from spreading. Wilson notes, though, that cost and infringement on civil liberties might deter nations from adopting testing and containment strategies. Do you think at-risk populations should submit to mandatory testing in order to bring this deadly disease to a halt? And should governments commit more money to conduct testing and teach prevention? Be sure to examine what is at stake for governments and society to adopt the path you advocate.

3. While Rita E. Carey shows concern over a supposed obesity epidemic among wealthier nations around the world, Patrick Basham and John Luik argue that statistics disprove that humans are getting fatter on average. Basham and Luik insist that health authorities' attempts to influence the public's diet are simply another example of government trying to control people's lives. Do you think Basham and Luik's claims are accurate, or do you believe that Carey and other professionals are correct in warning

against a potentially dangerous global trend? Support your response with evidence gained from the articles and any outside sources you find helpful.

Chapter 2

1. Mark Honigsbaum insists that, despite the low mortality rate from swine flu, the H1N1 virus could have been more deadly if governments had not taken the precautions and countermeasures they did. On the other hand, Daniel J. Ncayiyana maintains that the media and global health authorities hyped the threat of H1N1 for political reasons. Whose argument do you find more convincing? Why?

2. Karen DeCoster believes that politicians colluded with pharmaceutical companies to get rich off the hysteria surrounding the outbreak of H1N1 swine flu. How does Sam Vaknin refute this argument? Whose viewpoint do you believe is a more accurate assessment of the swine flu controversy? Explain why.

3. Based on the evidence presented in this chapter's viewpoints and any outside reading you have done, do you think the World Health Organization acted responsibly in declaring H1N1 a pandemic and calling upon governments to invest in expensive treatments? Explain what criteria you used to make up your mind on the matter.

Chapter 3

1. What kind of evidence does the writer of the Associated Press article cite in support of those who argue that vaccines are potentially dangerous? What argumentative strategy do Brenda L. Bartlett and Stephen K. Tyring utilize to claim that vaccines are beneficial to human health? Whose argument do you think is more convincing? Does your response reflect the way in which the author or authors presented the arguments? Explain.

2. Various media outlets have aired the assertion that vaccines may be accountable for the rise in autism among America's infants. How reasonable do you find this argument? What evidence do you think points conclusively to the acceptance or refutation of this supposed connection between vaccines and autism? Examine the viewpoints in this chapter as well as outside reading to support your claim.

3. Sherri Tenpenny insists that vaccine refusal should be the right of every person because forced immunization deprives people of their right to protect their own health as they see fit. Saad B. Omer and his colleagues maintain that vaccination has kept many virulent diseases at bay and that the benefits to society as a whole should not be overturned by a fearful minority. Explain your opinion on the debate between widespread vaccination and the right to safeguard one's own health. Is there a way to resolve the debate without jeopardizing public health and safety?

Chapter 4

1. Stephen E. Flynn and Irwin Redlener warn that the United States is not prepared for a major pandemic. According to these authors, what shortcomings exist in America's readiness? What remedies do they propose? What reasons can you think of for the lack of preparation in some of the areas Flynn and Redlener cite?

2. Tara O'Toole believes America is not ready for a bioterrorism attack. Aaron Katz, Andrea B. Staiti, and Kelly L. McKenzie, however, insist the country has learned some lessons and is improving its capacity to contend with such a threat. What evidence does each viewpoint give to support its argument? Whose opinion do you find more convincing? Explain why.

3. After reading John Barry's viewpoint, do you think his argument that nations are still not working cooperatively

in the face of pandemics is justified? Can you find instances in which nations have worked collectively to control diseases in recent decades? Explain your response to Barry's claim.

Organizations to Contact

The editors have compiled the following list of organizations concerned with the issues debated in this book. The descriptions are derived from materials provided by the organizations. All have publications or information available for interested readers. The list was compiled on the date of publication of the present volume; the information provided here may change. Be aware that many organizations take several weeks or longer to respond to inquiries, so allow as much time as possible.

AIDS Action
1424 K St. NW, Ste. 200, Washington, DC 20005
(202) 408-4848 • fax: (202) 408-1818
e-mail: information@aidsaction.org
website: www.aidsaction.org

Founded in 1984, AIDS Action seeks to provide a voice for the AIDS epidemic and facilitate AIDS policy change in the US government. The organization offers a wide range of information about HIV and provides treatment as well as coping methods for those living with or affected by the virus. In addition, AIDS Action works closely with research organizations to develop more effective treatments and to try to find a cure for the disease. AIDS Action is also an advocacy group working to establish preventative programs that stop the spread of AIDS. The organization's website provides a publications archive where visitors can read through fact sheets, policy briefs, and prevention assessments.

American Heart Association
7272 Greenville Ave., Dallas, TX 75231
(800) 242-8721
website: www.heart.org

The American Heart Association is dedicated to helping Americans live healthy lives without worry about cardiovascular disease and stroke. To do so, the organization makes extensive suggestions about healthy living, focusing on areas such as nutrition, stress management, physical activity, weight management, and smoking cessation. The American Heart Association offers numerous fact sheets about the risk factors of heart disease, general information about heart disease and stroke, and cookbooks supporting a healthy lifestyle.

American Public Health Association (APHA)

800 I St. NW, Washington, DC 20001-3710
(202) 777-APHA • fax: (202) 777-2534
website: www.apha.org

Founded in 1872, APHA is an organization of public health officials dedicated to improving public health for Americans through community-based health promotion and disease prevention. The organization works at the local and national levels advocating policy implementation to ensure that Americans have access to necessary health information and care. APHA publishes the peer-reviewed *American Journal of Public Health* and the newspaper the *Nation's Health*, which provide information about public health advances for health professionals, policy leaders, and the public.

American Red Cross

2025 E St. NW, Washington, DC 20006
(202) 303-5000
website: www.redcross.org

The American Red Cross has been working since 1881 to respond to emergencies both in the United States and around the world. The American Red Cross, in cooperation with International Red Cross organizations, has focused much effort on halting the HIV/AIDS pandemic by providing information about the disease and how it spreads to those in areas most affected by the virus. Additionally, the Red Cross has worked to ensure that those who have been infected with the virus have access to current treatment methods. The American Red Cross publishes the *HIV/AIDS Fact Book*, which is available by mail from local chapters nationwide.

Centers for Disease Control and Prevention (CDC)

1600 Clifton Rd., Atlanta, GA   30333
(800) 232-4636
e-mail: cdcinfo@cdc.gov
website: www.cdc.gov

CDC is a health agency within the US government's Department of Health and Human Services. The organization was founded in 1946 to find methods to control malaria. While its goals have since broadened, preventing and managing communicable and noncommunicable diseases remains a primary focus of the CDC. To do so, the organization offers guidelines for both professionals and the general public that suggest methods of slowing and preventing the spread of infectious disease. The CDC website also provides comprehensive information concerning the administration of vaccines, possible future pandemics, and healthy living tips to prevent disease.

Department of Health and Human Services (HHS)

200 Independence Ave. SW, Washington, DC   20201
(877) 696-6775
website: www.hhs.gov

HHS is the primary health agency within the US government concerned with Americans' health and well-being. Both the CDC and the National Institutes of Health fall under HHS control. While HHS provides a multitude of services to the American people, disease prevention and immunization constitute a top priority of the agency. As such, many HHS programs focus on researching new methods to combat disease and informing the public about things they can do to aid in the fight against disease. Flu.gov is the HHS website dedicated to providing the public with information about the safety of flu vaccinations as well as easy steps individuals can take to help limit or prevent flu outbreaks in their hometowns.

Every Child By Two (ECBT)

1100 G St. NW, Ste. 202, Washington, DC   20005-3806
(202) 783-7034 • fax: (202) 783-7042

e-mail: info@ecbt.org
website: www.ecbt.org

Founded by former First Lady Rosalynn Carter and Betty Bumpers in 1991, Every Child By Two is a national organization that seeks to inform parents about the need for early childhood vaccinations in order to curb mortality from preventable diseases. The organization also actively enlists the support of lawmakers and other politicians to spread the word about the personal and social benefits of vaccination. ECBT's website provides information for parents and news on topical issues.

The Global Health Council

1111 Nineteenth St. NW, Ste. 1120, Washington, DC   20036
(202) 833-5900 • fax: (202) 833-0075
website: www.globalhealth.org

A US-based membership organization, the Global Health Council seeks to inform both global and local government agencies and individuals about significant international health concerns in order to improve the health of individuals around the world. The council offers publications on a variety of topics, including *Global Health Magazine* which is available in both print and online formats, the *Global Health Opportunities* report, and multiple policy and research briefs and fact sheets about global health issues.

Immunization Action Coalition

1573 Selby Ave., Saint Paul, MN   55104
(651) 647-9009 • fax: (651) 647-9131
e-mail: admin@immunize.org
website: www.immunize.org

The Immunization Action Coalition works to increase immunization rates and to prevent disease by creating and distributing educational materials for health professionals and the public that enhance the delivery of safe and effective immunization services. The organization distributes immunization charts as well as publications for medical professionals in hopes of keeping immunization rates high.

The Obesity Society

8630 Fenton St., Ste. 814, Silver Spring, MD   20910
(301) 563-6526 • fax: (301) 563-6595
website: www.obesity.org

The Obesity Society is a scientific society that focuses its efforts on studying the causes and treatments of obesity and informing both the medical community and the public about any new findings concerning this epidemic. The organization also serves as an advocacy group for those affected by obesity. The Obesity Society's website provides publications such as obesity fact sheets, statistics, the *National Heart, Lung & Blood Institute's Obesity Guidelines*, and *The Practical Guide: Identification, Evaluation, and Treatment of Overweight and Obesity in Adults*. The official journal of the Obesity Society is *Obesity*.

Parents Requesting Open Vaccine Education (PROVE)

PO Box 91566, Austin, TX   78709-1566
(512) 288-3999
website: http://vaccineinfo.net

PROVE is a national organization that provides information on vaccination policies and practices. The purpose of the organization is to prevent vaccine injury and death and to inform parents and other individuals about their rights regarding vaccination so that they can make the best decisions to protect themselves and their families. The organization publishes a free online newsletter that provides immediate notifications of new developments regarding vaccines.

Think Twice Global Vaccine Institute

PO Box 9638, Santa Fe, NM   87504
(505) 983-1856
e-mail: think@thinktwice.com
website: www.thinktwice.com

Think Twice was founded in 1996 as an offshoot of New Atlantean Press, a publisher of books on holistic living. It disseminates information on vaccination topics to help parents make informed decisions concerning the necessity and safety of vaccines. It strongly supports the individual's right to refuse vaccination. The Think Twice website provides articles, studies, and personal stories about vaccine refusal.

World Health Organization (WHO)

525 Twenty-Third St. NW, Washington, DC   20037
(202) 974-3000 • fax: (202) 974-3663
e-mail: postmaster@paho.org
website: www.who.int

The WHO was established in 1948 as an agency within the United Nations with the purpose of establishing and securing a world where all people can enjoy high levels of mental and physical health. The organization conducts research and publishes information on a variety of methods to prevent and treat diseases such as malaria, SARS, and AIDS. Additionally, noncommunicable diseases such as obesity, cancer, and cardiovascular disease are addressed in WHO research and literature. WHO publications include the *Bulletin of the World Health Organization* and the *Pan American Journal of Public Health*, both available online. The Pan American Health Organization is the regional arm of the WHO with an office in the United States.

Bibliography of Books

Arthur Allen   *Vaccine: The Controversial Story of
                    Medicine's Greatest Lifesaver.* New
                    York: Norton, 2007.

Tony Barnett and   *AIDS in the Twenty-First Century:
Alan Whiteside   Disease and Globalization.* 2nd ed.;
                    fully revised and updated. New York:
                    Palgrave Macmillan, 2002.

John M. Barry   *The Great Influenza: The Story of the
                    Deadliest Pandemic in History.* New
                    York: Penguin, 2005.

David P. Clark   *Germs, Genes, & Civilization: How
                    Epidemics Shaped Who We Are Today.*
                    Upper Saddle River, NJ: Pearson,
                    2010.

Madeline Drexler   *Emerging Epidemics: The Menace of
                    New Infections.* New York: Penguin,
                    2003.

Helen Epstein   *The Invisible Cure: Why We Are
                    Losing the Fight Against AIDS in
                    Africa.* New York: Picador, 2007.

Laurie Garrett   *Betrayal of Trust: The Collapse of
                    Global Public Health.* New York:
                    Hyperion, 2001.

John Iliffe   *The African AIDS Epidemic: A
                    History.* Athens: Ohio University
                    Press, 2006.

Maryn McKenna   *Superbug: The Fatal Menace of
                    MRSA.* New York: Free Press, 2010.

Joseph Mercola
with Pat Killeen

*The Great Bird Flu Hoax: The Truth
They Don't Want You to Know About
the "Next Big Pandemic."* Nashville:
Thomas Nelson, 2009.

Neil Z. Miller

*Vaccines: Are They Really Safe and
Effective?* Santa Fe, NM: New
Atlantean, 2008.

Richard E.
Neustadt and
Harvey Fineberg

*The Epidemic That Never Was:
Policy-Making and the Swine Flu
Scare.* New York: Vintage, 1983.

Gary Null

AIDS: A Second Opinion. New York:
Seven Stories, 2002.

Michael B.A.
Oldstone

*Viruses, Plagues, and History: Past,
Present, and Future.* Rev. ed. New
York: Oxford University Press, 2010.

Dan Olmsted and
Mark Blaxil

*The Age of Autism: Mercury,
Medicine, and a Man-Made Epidemic.*
New York: Thomas Dunne, 2010.

Abigail A. Salyers
and Dixie D.
Whitt

*Revenge of the Microbes: How
Bacterial Resistance Is Undermining
the Antibiotic Miracle.* Washington,
DC: ASM, 2005.

Jessica Snyder
Sachs

*Good Germs, Bad Germs: Health and
Survival in a Bacterial World.* New
York: Hill and Wang, 2007.

Alan Sipress

*The Fatal Strain: On the Trail of
Avian Flu and the Coming Pandemic.*
New York: Viking, 2009.

Michael Specter   *Denialism: How Irrational Thinking Hinders Scientific Progress, Harms the Planet, and Threatens Our Lives*. New York: Penguin, 2009.

Brad Spellberg   *Rising Plague: The Global Threat from Deadly Bacteria and Our Dwindling Arsenal to Fight Them*. New York: Prometheus, 2009.

Sherri J. Tenpenny   *Saying No to Vaccines*. Middleburg Heights, OH: NMA Media, 2008.

Barry E. Zimmerman and David J. Zimmerman   *Killer Germs*. Chicago: Contemporary Books, 2003.

Index